A FIRE TO BE KINDLED

'A child's mind is not a vessel to be filled
but a fire to be kindled'

Plutarch

A FIRE TO BE KINDLED

THE GLOBAL INFLUENCE OF CHRIST'S HOSPITAL ON SCIENCE EDUCATION

BY
GORDON VAN PRAAGH

CHRIST'S HOSPITAL
2003

© GORDON VAN PRAAGH 2003

First published privately in 2003 by the author
through Christ's Hospital
Horsham, West Sussex RH13 7YP

ISBN 0-9507843-6-2

Designed and produced by John Mitchell
Printed in Great Britain by
St Edmundsbury Press,
Bury St Edmunds

CONTENTS

LIST OF PLATES *vi*

FOREWORD *vii*
by Richard Poulton, Head Master of Christ's Hospital, 1987–1996

PREFACE *xi*

Introduction *xiii*
1 A letter from H. L. O. Flecker in Pakistan 1
2 The *virus heuristicum Armstrongii* 4
3 Feedback from Old Blue scientists and engineers 15
4 Views from some science teachers 32
5 J. E. Morpurgo publishes *Chemistry by Discovery* 43
6 'Why don't you just tell us, sir?' 44
7 The Nuffield Science Teaching Project 53
8 Australia wants to know 62
9 'Guided Discovery' goes to Iran 68
10 School Science in Sarawak and Singapore 73
11 CREDO and CEDO 79
12 CREDO's first Curriculum Development Project – East Africa 83
13 'Science by Discovery' throughout Malaysia 90
14 Improvised laboratories for Chemistry by Discovery 99
15 The Nitty Gritty – extracts from a report to CEDO 101
16 Centenary Day at Christ's Hospital 106
References 110
List of subscribers 111
Index 112

PLATES

Extracts from C.H. boys' notebooks, 1902 page 10
Order for a keg of sea water page 12

between pages 82 and 83

1 H. L. O. Flecker and his Head of Science, A. R. Quraishi
2 Professor Henry E. Armstrong
3 Charles E. Browne. 'The right man to take charge of the Science School'
4 Quraishi introduced me to staff and pupils (in their ceremonial turbans) at Aichison College, Lahore, as coming from 'the world famous Science School of Christ's Hospital'
5 Collage of E.A.S.S.P. books
6 Cover of the Science Journal
7 The ruins of the palaces of the Kings of Persia dating back to the 5th century BC
8 Walking to school from a kampong
9 The Law of the Lever. A student in Zambia wonders how a small weight can lift a heavier one
10 Tan Sri Dato (Dr) Haji Hamdan, Director General of Education, Malaysia, 1969
11 The British tutors and Malaysian teachers in a Curriculum Development Course in Malaysia
12 My team of tutors for the Malaysian Project
13 Science teachers attending a Malaysia Curriculum Development Course
14 From the film Learning Science in Malaysia
15 'Chemistry by Discovery' in Malaysia
16 The Chief Minister visiting the School Science Exhibition
17 Teaching chemistry as I did half a century ago

FOREWORD
BY
RICHARD POULTON
Head Master of Christ's Hospital 1987–1996

A GOOD SCHOOLMASTER (and, of course, a good schoolmistress – my use of the masculine must be read as covering both) has many attributes. I apologise for the apparent political incorrectness in that first sentence. I could have escaped the difficulty by using the word 'teacher', but I believe that there is a subtle difference between 'teachers' and 'schoolmasters' (and 'schoolmistresses'). There is an implication in the latter words, not just of a job, not just of a worthy and noble profession, but also of a whole way of life and of a guiding philosophy. Gordon Van Praagh was definitely 'a good schoolmaster', embodying those extra dimensions with a zeal that longevity has not diminished.

Let me start again. A good schoolmaster has many attributes. He may be wise in his discipline and strong in his pastoral gifts. He may have a gift of humour or a magnetic personality or 'the common touch' that binds him to his pupils and vice versa. He may have the brain of a near-Einstein or the cover-drive of a David Gower or the musical talent of a great performer. But there are two attributes that a good schoolmaster *must* possess if he is really going to merit the accolade. He must love his subject for its own sake, and he must delight in that wonderful sense of achievement when he knows that he has passed on some deep element of knowledge or, more importantly, of real understanding. His purpose and his reward is to make the eyes of his pupil light up, first with intellectual curiosity and then with comprehension. To kindle the fire is the mission of a good schoolmaster.

This book tells the story of how Armstrong and Browne established a new scientific approach at Christ's Hospital, and of how one man became their evangelist, carrying the gospel of the heuristic method literally around the world. It records the impact of the method and the man, on a number of his pupils who became distinguished scientists and then on a much wider world.

There is a strange degree of symmetry within Dr Gordon Van Praagh's overseas career. When H. L. O. Flecker retired from the headship of Christ's Hospital and became Principal of Lawrence College in Pakistan, it was to Gordon that he turned for help with his science laboratories. It was through A. R. Quraishi that much of that help was transmitted. Forty years later, Mr Quraishi came back to the Head Master's study in Christ's Hospital, to ask whether the then Head Master would consider starting a new English-style school in Pakistan. It was an offer that after due consideration I turned down – but two years after that, as I laboured in vain to explain certain things to the Thai owner of a school that I was founding south of Bangkok, it was a meeting that I remembered. It prompted me to recall that there was one man who had more experience of understanding the problems and the potential of building laboratories in Third World countries and in the Far East than anyone else. Gordon was due to come to Penang, and it was not difficult to tempt him to come further north, to explain what was really needed in a new laboratory, and why (and in some aspects, how!). That he was in his late 80s was no hindrance to his perception, his analysis and his powers of persuasion. The layout plans were amended and the orders for equipment were modified. It was actually thirty-three years since Gordon had left the C.H. staff, but he was still preaching the same message, with the confidence that came from knowing that academically and intellectually, it was the right one.

By identifying my problems in Thailand with those of one of my C.H. predecessors when he was in Pakistan, I relate very much to the first chapter of this book. But I also relate to the last chapter, because I was able to witness Dr Van Praagh's 'Centenary of Science' lesson at C.H. in 2002. He did not know that I was there. He refers to the adults who 'stood at the back', but I stood in the doorway, at the front, *behind* Gordon and therefore facing the pupils. From there I could watch the expressions of the youngsters as they picked their way along a pathway of experiment and observation, reason and response. The message and the magic were still in the man. The pupils were there 'to learn, not to memorise'. (In fairness it must be said that the heuristic tradition had never died in C.H. in those intervening years, despite the encroachment of unprecedented examination pressures.)

When a visitor stands in the Quadrangle of Christ's Hospital and considers the surrounding buildings, he or she is likely to identify correctly the Victorian essential elements of Dining Hall, Chapel and Big School. But what subject would occupy the classrooms that they planned on the fourth side? What in the 1890s carried enough weight to have such a prime position? Classics, the most prestigious of the academic subjects at the time? English? Not Modern Languages, of course, for the world with which Englishmen came into contact was expected to speak English. Perhaps the classrooms might harbour the Royal Mathematical School, a jewel in the C.H. crown?

No contemporary observer would have expected Science, a subject that had only been approved for the C.H. curriculum by the Royal Commission within that very decade. That first daring decision was the legacy of Professor Henry Armstrong, who brought about the decision to build the laboratories in the prime position where they still stand. Charles Browne was the man who built up the practice of the heuristic method. He converted many of the doubters, and with the benefit of his teaching philosophy, large numbers of Old Blues went on to distinguished scientific careers.

Gordon Van Praagh was not an Old Blue – but he was tutored by Browne at the London Day Training College after Browne had theoretically 'retired'. He caught the *virus heuristicum Armstrongii*, and has transmitted it ever since. He has had an impact on the teaching of science in many different parts of the world, sometimes through the teamwork of such enterprises as the Nuffield project, and sometimes through his own enterprise. It is no surprise to learn that he has been honoured with the rank of *Dato* in Malaysia for his services to science education.

This book is just a small part of *his* story, as well as an indication of how much C.H. has contributed to science teaching around the world.

PREFACE

THIS BOOK CELEBRATES the centenary of the teaching of science in the new laboratories at Christ's Hospital, Horsham. When I was asked to write it, I was reluctant to do so, firstly because I was only seven years away from my own centenary and secondly because my career had been such that I would have to be writing a good deal about myself. My old friend and adviser, Tony Mansell, said 'Forget your false modesty and get on with it! You are the only person whose experience enables you to do it'. So I did, and so enjoyed doing it that I finished the first draft in four months.

I had difficulty in choosing a title. My ideas on education mostly came from my 'Dip.Ed.' year. The chemistry tutor was Charles E. Browne, who expounded the ideas of a Professor Armstrong on the 'heuristic' method of teaching chemistry. But I was most influenced by Sir Percy Nunn, Professor of Education, whose quotation from Plutarch defined our basic attitudes to education:

'A child's mind is not a vessel to be filled but a fire to be kindled'.

That was it!

In spite of the somewhat subjective contribution to the views offered from time to time on the 'discovery method', I hope the book will form a useful contribution to educational research into the effectiveness of different methods of teaching science. It traces the extended influence of Christ's Hospital science education in the following scheme:

(i) The influence on the pupils and their careers (Chapters 2–6).
(ii) The influence spreads through the Nuffield Science Teaching Project (Chapters 7 and 8);
(iii) and overseas through British Council courses (Chapters 1, 9 and 10);

(iv) and through the Centre for Educational Development Overseas to Curriculum Development Projects in East Africa and Malaysia (Chapters 11–13).

There are many who helped me to compile this book. First and foremost I am extremely grateful to my old pupil Trevor Hoskins, who edited most of the text and greatly improved it. The illustrations owe their excellence to the skills of Michael Guest, an expert enhancer of archive material; to him I owe much useful advice. The publishing and indexing skills of John and Susan Mitchell have been indispensable and they have been generous with their time. Without the keen support of two other Old Blues, Lance Reynolds and Peter Bloomfield, the book could not have been produced – Peter saw it through the process of publication, and he and Lance not only raised the finance required (mostly from other Old Blues) but encouraged me every step of the way.

I want to record my warmest thanks to Richard Poulton, Head Master of Christ's Hospital from 1987–1996, for his very kind and generous Foreword. I'm glad he has recovered from the shock of my visit to him when he was starting up a new residential school in the midst of a coconut plantation in southern Thailand, an almost impossible task – especially if you don't speak Thai!

My one-time secretary, Fiona Potter, again applied her skills to interpreting my handwriting, as did Mrs Adams and Mrs Bourton, and produced faultless typescripts.

Finally, I want to say thank you to my friendly neighbours, Colin and Ann, Bob and Jean, Jack and Sue, for all their help in enabling me to carry on my normal life while writing this book.

INTRODUCTION

'H. E. Armstrong and C. E. Browne. Oh dear, not again!.' said my secretary, 'I'm fed up with Argumentative old Armstrong and Boring old Browne!' 'Really, Fiona, you must not refer to two of the most distinguished figures in the history of education in that manner!'

But maybe she had a point – anyone interested in education will know something about Armstrong and Browne. This book is concerned with something that very few people know anything about, so why not take the plunge and return to Armstrong and Browne later on?

CHAPTER 1

A LETTER FROM H. L. O. FLECKER IN PAKISTAN

WHEN FLECKER RETIRED from being Head Master of Christ's Hospital in 1955 he said to me 'I don't want to be put on the shelf yet and have accepted the offer to become Principal of Lawrence College in the Murree Hills, Pakistan'. After he had been at Lawrence College a year, he wrote to me about their laboratories: 'They are not bad, but the Bunsen burners don't work'. He wanted me to go out and help his science staff to get things going properly. He then sent his head physicist over to England to spend a term at Christ's Hospital. His name was A. R. Quraishi and he proved a very popular member of the Common Room. I well remember the time when a colleague asked him: 'Has Mr Flecker learnt Urdu – I expect he is too old to learn a new language?' 'Not at all' replied Quraishi, 'Mr Flecker is not too old for anything!' And that was a pretty good estimate of the man; he involved himself in all aspects of life in the school. But he was no scientist and so wanted my help in the science department at Lawrence College (plate 1).

In the late 1950s and on into the 1960s and 1970s, the sponsoring of courses for science teachers in developing countries was part of the efforts of the British Council to spread British culture overseas. Among other specialists, such as surgeons, footballers and ballet dancers, they included science teachers in their 'Specialist Tours'. Flecker was able to persuade the Council in Karachi to request a Specialist Tour in the teaching of science which would include a course to be held at Lawrence College. They agreed, provided the teachers from other schools in West Pakistan could also attend. One of the other schools was Aitchison College, Lahore, quite a famous independent school, founded in 1886 for the sons of princes, but later with a broader intake. (I was to visit Aitchison College again thirty-seven years later.) About fifteen teachers attended my course in Lawrence College. It lasted two weeks, and besides giving the usual lectures and holding discussions afterwards, I borrowed a class of schoolboys and gave some science lessons in front of the teachers.

My first lesson went something like this: I picked up a white piece of rock from the path on which I was walking towards the lecture room. The lesson was to be a special occasion, because, in addition to the teachers, a class of pupils was to be sitting in front and an Inspector of Education at the back. The teachers seemed to be rather in awe of him – but the pupils didn't know who he was. The main object of my course was to try to show the teachers that science could be taught in other ways than by lecturing, learning by heart and examinations. At this time efforts were being made not only to modernise school science but to improve teaching methods. Pupils were encouraged to ask questions, to think for themselves and to discover and find out – both in the laboratory and in books. This was very different from the way science had been taught – especially in Asia.

To start the lesson I asked the class what they thought this piece of white rock might be. They had already studied chemistry for a couple of years and had heard of limestone. Before any of them could reply the Inspector shouted from the back, 'It is silica!' 'Thank you', I said and, to the class, 'The Inspector says it is silica. Can you think of anything else it might be? Could it be something you have already studied?' One shy response came, 'Could it be limestone?' 'Maybe' I said, 'But how can we tell? Can you think of a reaction of limestone that you know about which we could use as a test?' After more such heavy-going discussion, we decided to add a few drops of acid to the stone: if it were limestone it would 'fizz' as the carbon dioxide gas came off; if it were silica it wouldn't. I got a pupil to come forward and carry out the test in front of the class. There was a lot of bubbling on the stone, easily visible to all the class. The Inspector had been wrong. I felt very sorry for him and embarrassed that he would lose face, but I had to say, 'Well, it looks as if the Inspector was wrong'. (A pity he shouted out in the first place!)

It is interesting to note that, while I was staying with Flecker he showed me a book he had written entitled *A Book of General Knowledge*. The first words of the Preface read 'This is not a science textbook but an English textbook'. However, most of the content consisted of mini-biographies of famous scientists – it came as a great surprise to me that Flecker, the classicist, could write on such a subject, especially as the number of reference books he had with him in Pakistan was limited. I had forgotten what Quraishi had said about him. This was his contribution to science education in Pakistan, and although printed on poor paper Flecker had put a great effort into writing it and I found it a fascinating read. His daughter Philippa has the original copy in her possession in Australia, and kindly provided this list of chapter headings for me:

1. Air
2. Breathing and Barometers
3. Galileo Galilei
4. The Universe
5. Sir Isaac Newton
6. Water
7. Water Supply
8. Heat
9. Health
10. Louis Pasteur

My second visit to Pakistan was in 1996. Quraishi had then become the Principal of Aitchison College and he wrote saying 'I want you to come out here and improve the teaching of science in my school'. The prospect was daunting – how would an experienced teaching staff react to the visit of a total stranger telling them how to do their job better? I would have to be tactful! However, it turned out that the staff were very friendly and co-operative and we had many informal discussions. I was given an effusive welcome before the whole school of over 2,000 pupils in the open-air arena. Quraishi introduced me as coming from 'the world famous Science School of Christ's Hospital' (plate 4). We discussed teaching through 'guided discovery' and I gave several lessons to illustrate the method. Quraishi also wanted advice on improving the laboratories and converting two 'science classrooms' so that they could also be used for simple experiments.

At the time of this visit, it so happened that a second large school was being planned for Lahore. I was asked to comment on the plans for the proposed science laboratories and was glad to have the opportunity of suggesting changes that would make them more suitable for teaching by 'guided discovery' methods.

CHAPTER 2

THE VIRUS HEURISTICUM ARMSTRONGII

'PROFESSOR HENRY EDWARD ARMSTRONG was one of the great scientists of the latter part of the 19th century. A chemist of world-wide eminence, he also became one of the leading educational reformers of his time' (plate 2). So wrote Charles E. Browne (plate 3), the first science teacher at Christ's Hospital, appointed in 1899. Browne owed a great deal to Armstrong and in 1954 he wrote an account of Armstrong's influence on the teaching of science.[1] An appreciation of the work of Browne himself was written in 1966 by Ernest H. Rodd, DSC, one of Charles E. Browne's first pupils, and bound together as one book with Browne's earlier account.[2] The following is a condensed paraphrase of Browne's description:

> Armstrong's interest in education was first awakened in 1870 when he was appointed lecturer in chemistry to first-year medical students at St Bartholomew's Hospital. He found these students utterly unable to interpret the simplest experimental results, or even to make adequate and correct notes of any chemical change they observed. He found no challenge by them to a statement, no desire for proof of an assertion, no critical spirit whatever. Their sole aim was to learn statements of fact, definitions and whatever could be stored in the memory for examinations. Armstrong found it impossible to build up a reasonable postgraduate course in view of such an attitude of mind. He had to devise the simplest type of elementary practical work before they could deal with the more complicated problems.
>
> His experience was repeated when he was appointed Professor of Chemistry at the London Institution at Finsbury in 1871 where he had to deal with students of a different type – mostly industrial and commercial. They proved equally unresponsive to Armstrong's efforts to get them to think for themselves. He realised that the cause of their unresponsiveness lay in the deficiencies of their school training. There was an absence of any idea

of training in scientific method and of practical experience through which alone training in scientific method is possible.

By 1890 Armstrong was launching his campaign for the adoption of the 'Heuristic' method of teaching. This was introduced by Meiklejohn in 1860 and was derived from the Greek work *Eureka*, meaning 'I have found out.' It was especially used in connection with a system of education under which the pupil is trained to find out things for himself. Any such revolutionary idea was bound to meet with opposition. Armstrong's critics interpreted it to mean that children should make new discoveries, whereas Armstrong used the word to mean 'a fact discovered by a person for himself – although well-known to many people, it is still a new discovery to him.' These misunderstandings led Armstrong to issue, in detailed form, his scheme for heuristic work in schools.

In 1891 Armstrong saw the possibility of carrying out a trial to show that the heuristic method was practicable and capable of being applied in an ordinary school. When the Royal Commission on Christ's Hospital published their report in that year they recommended, among other important changes, that science teaching should be a definite part of the curriculum. Armstrong was elected to be the Royal Society's representative on the Council of Almoners of the school and remained an active member for forty years.

Christ's Hospital, famous for its classical and mathematical traditions, still ignored the claims of science as a subject for serious study. Occasionally during the last years in London a few popular lessons in chemistry had been given to a senior class in the school by a visiting lecturer from the neighbouring hospital, and some experiments in physics attempted by some of the boys under the supervision of a mathematics master.

The so-called science room was a dark dingy place, and reminded one of a second-hand dealer's store of discarded lecture apparatus. Armstrong realised that the removal of the school to new premises in the country provided an opportunity to provide room and equipment for individual practical work by a large number of students and a chance to establish a system of heuristic teaching. The science building comprised four large rooms, 60 × 30 feet each, with a number of small rooms for stores and for masters' use. There were no classrooms as such – boys were not to be talked to – they were to do things. The large rooms were called Workshops as he considered the term 'laboratory' too academic. They were later named after the famous scientists Faraday, Cavendish, Dalton and Davy.

It was through Armstrong that I was offered the post of Science Master in 1899 when the school was still in London. He at once took me into his confidence, putting me in possession of his ideas for the new school at Horsham. Visiting the school during its building we found the walls and most of the flooring of the new science building complete and we set to work designing the working benches, water and gas supply, fume cupboards, sinks and other fittings.

The Science work throughout the school would be based on practical work by individual pupils. I decided to start by basing this on a particular topic that Armstrong had used for trying out his heuristic method with three of his own children at home. The question of dealing with a larger number of boys, moving about and talking, presented a great difficulty to many, but the boys became so interested in their work that the question of discipline did not arise.

Armstrong frequently visited the classes. Among other points we noted that it was unnecessary to use elaborately manufactured apparatus for the experiments. Wherever possible homemade equipment was employed. Tools and material were supplied; we even had an anvil and a forge, and made our own sensitive paper for printing plates of the apparatus. A sufficient number of balances were housed in dust-proof cases to allow each boy and his partner to carry out weighing operations.

The results of any experiment were always posted up on the blackboard in tabular form and used by the boys to check their results. At the conclusion of the practical work, the boys would assemble round the Master to discuss the results. There were no desks for the boys to sit at – they rested their notebooks on so-called 'stand rails' during the discussions. [A few stand rails were preserved in the Science School.]

Armstrong fully appreciated the need for small classes if the heuristic method was to have a chance to succeed. It was through his support and influence that the science staff was increased to keep the number of boys per master to sixteen as compared to twenty-five for other subjects. Practically the whole school attended science classes and the number of science masters had to be increased eventually to eight. Each class attended twice a week for one and half hours each time. Text books were not used in the ordinary way but were kept on shelves with other reference books. Boys' own notebooks became, so to speak, their text books.

As the new scheme of work matured the senior classes became sufficiently trained to study for university scholarships, largely by themselves. The Science Department soon became popular among many of the abler boys and the buildings, large as they were, could not cope. Again Armstrong showed his interest and plans were drawn up for an additional building to include biological laboratories, practical mathematics and geography rooms, a science lecture theatre and a science library. In due course, the new Science School was built and was opened by the Prince of Wales in 1929.

To sum up, Professor Henry Armstrong must be given the credit for having given to Christ's Hospital the opportunity, through the study of science, of increasing its pupils' powers of observation and criticism, and of encouraging them to become self-reliant, honest and sincere.

A bronze bust of Professor Armstrong is housed in the Science Library. It is a replica of one in the City and Guilds College and is a reminder of Professor Armstrong's great service to education generally and especially to Christ's Hospital.

Sir William Hamilton Fyfe, Head Master of Christ's Hospital from 1919 to 1930, wrote a sketch of Armstrong's work as a Prologue to Rodd's book. Part of it reads as follows:

> I first knew Professor Armstrong when I was appointed Head Master of Christ's Hospital in 1919. In the spring of that year I was summoned to appear before the ... Governing Body of the school and was told that I was the only candidate to be interviewed. I was therefore surprised to be kept waiting for more than an hour. I learned later that Professor Armstrong was all this time warning his colleagues against the appointment of a 'classic' and using every argument that he could find (and he could always find plenty) to induce them to choose a mathematician instead. His appeal was unsuccessful and I was appointed and supposed that I should find the Professor a thorn in my side. I was quite wrong. A few weeks later he invited me to lunch with him ... and we soon made friends, and I enjoyed the privilege of his friendship, advice and exhortation until I left Christ's Hospital in 1930.

> I found at Horsham many features of special excellence of which the most noticeable were the Science School, the Art School and the Manual School. Each of these was at that time unique and they owed their existence and the excellence of their planning to Armstrong's initiative and wisdom ... He secured the appointment of exactly the right men to take charge of these departments. Charles Browne ... was as great a pioneer as Armstrong. He fully shared the Professor's belief in the efficacy of the Heuristic Method, and successfully solved the very difficult problem of applying it in a school of over 800 boys. ...
>
> Browne organised the teaching of Science, trained his assistant masters and inspired his pupils at Christ's Hospital for twenty-seven years. His appointment was one of Armstrong's most notable services to the School. ... At first most of the other masters looked loftily askance at Browne ... but it was not long before the infection of the *virus heuristicum Armstrongii* spread to other subjects. Other masters began to abandon the belief that textbooks and their own voices were the only instruments of teaching and to devise methods in which their pupils could take an active part.
>
> Armstrong took a lively, paternal interest in all these developments. He visited us often, usually wearing loose tweeds dyed, rumour said, by his own hand (and of course by means of vegetable dyes) to a colour between that of an orange and a lemon. I always welcomed the sight of his stocky, bearded figure in this characteristic costume.

A large volume of Armstrong's writing was published in 1903[3] and a selection of his papers in 1973[4]. The papers were arranged in the chronological order of their original publication. As editor, I hoped to make this collection of use to teachers in training by quoting sections which seemed to bear on modern problems. These were set out as a series of topics for discussion. The list of contents of the 1910 edition was also included.

Writing in 1966, Rodd explained that boys coming to the school in 1899 may have wondered why there was a Ward (dormitory) XIV and a Ward XVI, but no Ward XV. This was because Ward XV had been adapted to be a laboratory. This is where Browne started to teach science in a small way in preparation for the expansion planned for the new school at Horsham. Rodd continued:

> Fortunately, one of Browne's private notebooks ... has been

preserved. ... The courses he envisaged are based on practical work by the boys, not formal lessons; work benches, not classrooms. The boys' activities were to be based on the desire to solve some problem by experiment, the problem must be simple enough to require very little experience and no elaborate apparatus. The teacher is to afford guidance and suggestion – mainly by questions – and should adopt the attitude of a co-enquirer, not an authority. ...These and similar notes ... reveal a man with a faith in his mission and determination to succeed. ... There is no doubt that the heuristic approach makes greater demands on the forethought and patience of the teacher than the formal, didactic method aptly termed 'chalk and talk'. ...

Looking back, as one who took part in the move from London to Horsham in May 1902, the writer can only marvel at the efficiency with which the operation was carried out. ... No-one can have had a busier time than Charles E. Browne during that Easter Holiday. Not only had the new laboratories to be prepared but a new Science Staff had to be briefed in revolutionary methods of teaching. ...

It soon became clear that older boys studying science subjects must be given a status in the school equivalent to that of boys studying the older subjects of classics and mathematics. 'Science Grecians' appeared on the scene, proudly wearing their buttons and velvet cuffs.... One of the earliest Science Grecians was (Dr) E. C. Williams. ... Unlike the writer, he went to science from the classical side, where science was regarded very much as an unimportant sideline. ... Grecians were expected to proceed to Oxford or Cambridge, but Williams gained a scholarship at Manchester University. ... Now living in the U.S.A., ... he wrote a long description of the science teaching in his time at Christ's Hospital to Professor Elgin ... at Princeton [in 1955]. Some of this is worth quoting. 'We had no textbooks; we dealt only with things we observed for ourselves, the experiments we had made and the deductions we were able to draw from what we had seen or measured. ... The only scientific works I remember reading before I was seventeen were the Alembic Club Reprints of papers which Chas. introduced me to with the remark that there I might learn how great minds had tackled problems. ... I think his idea was to let one see how brighter lads than we (Boyle, Harvey, Priestley, Lavoisier, Faraday, Davy and so on) would go about the kind of work we were doing. ...'

Browne's reign as Head of the Science School lasted for twenty-four sea. In this experiment I do not expect to use as much water, say about five litres (5,000 c.c.). But first you will want to know where we get the salt water. It is brought in kegs or small casks from Lowestoft by the Great Eastern Railway, and sold at a cost of 1½ᵈ per gallon, cheap enough for any one to have a salt water bath at home instead of having to go to the sea side for it. Having boiled this water down, and found that there was heaps more sediment in this five litres of salt water than in the ten litre of fresh, I continued boiling down till it became a pasty mass. There was a difficulty to filter the water there being such an amount of sediment. The ordinary way would take such a long time, so I had to use a filter pump. I boiled down this filtrate to about one third cooled and filtered, and left to crystallise if

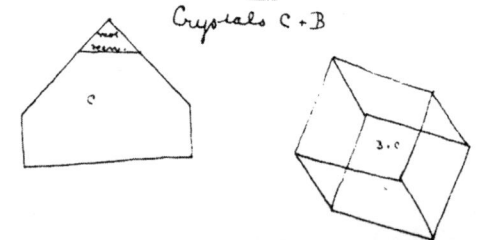

Crystals C + B

years after the removal to Horsham, during which time full recognition came of the importance of the subject in 20th century education. The war years, 1914–18, were a difficult period, during which Browne lost three of his more valuable colleagues, ... and suitable staff were not easy to obtain. Yet it was during this period that not only science but also engineering made definite progress in the school. ... Before Browne retired [in 1926] plans were already in hand to extend the science buildings which had become inadequate for the increasing number of boys studying science, especially if they were to be taught the subject as a practical discipline in the workshop rather than the classroom.

The new laboratories (now the New Science School) were opened by the Prince of Wales in 1929 after Browne's retirement.

Rodd's book also included the following description:
Record books
The carefully compiled records of experiments done were from the first considered of great importance. A few of the books have been preserved [and are now in the Christ's Hospital Archives, see opposite]. The earliest are remarkable for the copperplate handwriting in the tradition of the London Writing School. ... A later book, started in 1902 after the removal, still in the same style of writing, starts with an interesting description, accompanied by a carefully drawn plan, of the new laboratory, Faraday, contrasting it enthusiastically with the converted Ward in London in which science had first been studied.

One notebook from the London days records a series of experimental investigations undertaken by the boys which arose out of a statement in a story that Chas E. Browne had read to the class. The story was about a monkey which discovered that a large rock, too heavy to lift on land, could be lifted under the sea because, said the story, 'objects weigh less under water than in the air'. Charles Browne would say 'This is a silly story – most of it obviously untrue, but what about the statement that the rock weighed less under water than in the air? Is that true or not?' So of course the class were keen to find out and were well motivated to carry out the experiment – weighing some objects in air and under water. The note-

Extracts from C.H. boys' notebooks, 1902

books record their results and their delight in making the discovery that these were in agreement with the statement in the story.

One boy objected to the use of tap water, pointing out that the monkey had used sea water. (Did he know that he was leading the class on to the next experiment?) We have the order for the delivery at the back entrance of Christ's Hospital, Newgate Street, of a keg of sea water by the Great Eastern Railway. After using this for the weighing experiment, and finding that the rocks lost even more weight than they had in tap water, the class wanted to know why. They proceeded to evaporate ten litres of the sea water. They found that a number of white substances were precipitated, examined samples through a microscope and opened up the study of new areas of chemistry for investigation.

Order for a keg of sea water

Rodd then gives some comments from Old Blues 'who eventually became involved in science', and I have edited these as follows:

Sir Ewart Smith (1909–1916) who became a director of Imperial Chemical Industries: 'The essence of Chas.'s teaching was that boys had to find things out for themselves. My impression is that we did not cover a wide syllabus and thank God I never had to take an external exam. Judging from my experience of young graduates in the past twenty-five years I feel that they have covered far more ground than we did but their understanding of principles tends to be less. Their initiative and critical faculties have not been well developed.'

A. S. C. Lawrence who was under Browne in 1916–17 said that he made chemistry interesting to him and gave him the feeling that it made sense. Lawrence became well known for his researches on the surface properties of liquids and was eventually Professor of Physical Chemistry at Sheffield University.

Another of Browne's first pupils was Barnes Wallis, who later became a distinguished aeronautical engineer responsible for the structure of the Wellington bomber, the development of the 'bouncing bomb' and the pioneer work in developing the swing-wing technique used in many aircraft designs, particularly Concorde. Of Charles E. Browne's lessons, Barnes Wallis wrote 'A chemistry lesson with "Uncle Chas" was more like a lesson in logic and understanding than a lesson in the facts of chemistry.'

The spread of Armstrong's ideas is in large part due to Charles E. Browne. When he retired at the age of sixty he was still young in spirit and full of energy. He was soon appointed to a post at the London Day Training College where university graduates studied for a year for the Diploma in Education. Browne was tutor to the science students of whom I was one. In 1933 he spent a year as lecturer at St John's University, Shanghai. He returned to the London College where he continued to supervise student teachers until he was nearly seventy years old. A lecture on the heuristic method was given at the College annually and a party of their students visited Christ's Hospital every year to see the present form of 'heurism' in action.

In 1954 I wondered what Professor Armstrong would say if he visited Christ's Hospital then. He would have seen considerable changes in the layout and equipment of the laboratories and in the method of teaching. Although he might not recognise his heuristic method in its present form yet I was sure he would realise that the essence of his teaching method had endured and that the heuristic spirit pervaded the teaching of science, not only at Christ's Hospital but in many schools throughout the country. Summing up, I continued:

> A frequent theme of many of Her Majesty's Inspectors is that pupils should learn science at first hand in the laboratory, not only from textbooks, and this emphasis permeates the vacation courses they run for science teachers. However, it would be wrong to give the impression that the heuristic method is practised today as Charles Browne practised it earlier in the century. It is an attitude that has survived, a manner of approach to science teaching – the realisation of the importance of allowing the pupils to take part in a quest. The emotion aroused by some little discovery makes memory effortless and releases energy which carries the explorer on to fresh fields of investigation.

Today there are two main factors that make it difficult to practise the heuristic method: the predominance of examinations and the increased size of classes. With regard to the latter, we at Christ's Hospital are fortunate: the legacy from Armstrong and C. E. Browne and his successor D. H. Burleigh is enshrined in the generous provision of laboratory space, and the classes have been kept relatively small by the appointment of the necessary staff. Although small classes are ideal, large ones are not necessarily a bar to the use of the heuristic approach. Much can be done through demonstration experiments in which members of the class take part.

The difficulty of having to study many topics in order to cover an examination syllabus can be overcome along the following lines. Although it is impossible to be 100 per cent heuristic all the time (one wonders if it ever was!) it is quite possible to make a heuristic study of small parts of the syllabus. These 'heuristic patches' fertilise the rest of the work. (I owe this metaphor to John Bradley, who taught at Christ's Hospital from 1933–36 and contributed much to the heuristic way in which we taught chemistry.)

The heuristic patches may vary in duration from, say, one to four weeks, and there might be several of them during the year. Their frequency decreases as one goes from the lower to the higher forms, but by the time a pupil has had two or three years of science study in this manner, he has caught the spirit of the approach and realises what sort of experimentation, hypothesizing and reasoning lie behind the bald statements of the textbook. He has also learnt how to find this out for himself and is able to set about his practical work and his reading in a business-like manner.

When the heuristic approach is used, the ground covered is, of course, less than that where the teaching methods are didactic. Later on the situation is reversed; the older pupils are building on a sounder foundation than those who have covered more ground learnt largely from textbooks.

CHAPTER 3

FEEDBACK FROM OLD BLUE SCIENTISTS AND ENGINEERS

FIVE OF CHARLES E. BROWNE'S ex-pupils became Fellows of the Royal Society. Proud of their achievement, Barnes Wallis gave a dinner party for them in the early sixties. They were:

Professor P. Hall, elected 1942. Mathematician, at C.H. 1915–22;
Dr Barnes Wallis, elected 1945. Engineer, at C.H. 1900–1906;
Professor K. C. T. Franklin, elected 1955. Physiologist, at C.H. 1908–16;
Sir Ewart Smith, elected 1957. Director of ICI, at C.H. 1909–16;
Dr L. H. Gray, elected 1961. Director of the British Empire Cancer Campaign Research Unit in Radiobiology, at C.H. 1918–24.

Not long afterwards the youngest of them, L. H. Gray, died at the age of sixty. A memoir published by the Royal Society described him as a maker of scientific history, and gave some details of his formative years at Christ's Hospital.[5]

> He went first to Latimer School from which at the age of thirteen he won a scholarship to Christ's Hospital. . . . In the classroom at school, science was his consuming joy. . . . The masters at Christ's Hospital who had a special influence on him were Chas. Browne (Head of Science), and Hyde ('Dido') who instructed him in maths and was later his House Master. He was very fond of both. Browne was especially important to him for several reasons. He found himself behindhand in actual chemical knowledge, and Chas. Browne encouraged him to 'catch up' by doing experiments at home in the holidays. Also, Browne was cultured, and had wide horizons which were specially displayed in his home on Sunday evenings where meetings of the 'Philosophical Society' (for Science Grecians) were held and the boys were served tea and cakes by Mrs Browne.

I wondered how many of those who had left Christ's Hospital more recently had attained such distinction. I therefore wrote to about forty Old Blues who had distinguished themselves in their scientific careers and tried to find out from them the names of others. This showed that three were Fellows of the Royal Society: Professor D. G. Northcott, mathematician, at C.H. 1927–35; Professor Sir Christopher Zeeman, mathematician, Oxford University, at C.H. 1939–43; and Professor Keith Bowen, scientist, at C.H. 1951–59. Many others had gained other worthwhile awards. I asked them to record their recollections of their time spent in studying science at Christ's Hospital and the effect they thought it had had on them and their careers, and these were recorded in *The Teaching of Science at Christ's Hospital Since 1900AD*.[6] More Old Blues were contacted in 2003, and extracts from their views on the influence that C.H. Science has had on them follow below. As one might expect, there is a lot of repetition – nearly all contributors pay tribute to the benefits of studying science by a 'discovery method' derived from Armstrong's heuristic method. For example, one contributor says: 'The general approach to the subject, based on the heuristic method, was stimulating and strengthened my determination to be a scientist'. Another says: 'The heuristic method taught me to think for myself'. Another wrote: 'The teaching of science at C.H. was of quite inestimable value to me. It laid the foundation of my scientific career'.

Some of the Old Blue contributors mention some unusual events which I think are worthy of comment. For example, Professor Anderson recalls that his hobby of making plaster casts of animal footprints, leaves and even the face of one of his peers may have suggested to him his career in dentistry. I was his junior housemaster and I well remember his asking me about his career. I had recently been given a book called *Square Pegs in Round Holes*. For each career discussed there were two columns, one listing the requirements of the career and the other asking questions about the candidate's interests and abilities. We answered the questions and included under 'hobbies' that he enjoyed making plaster casts. The book then pointed him towards a career in dentistry.

Professor McLean wrote:
> I tried unsuccessfully to make mustard gas and, successfully, to make styrene, and nearly set fire to the laboratory. VP stood back and let me try. I think he knew enough about what I was doing to stop disasters, but I suspect that no seventeen-year-old is allowed

to do such things nowadays.

He is right – risk taking is something we seem to abhor, and yet we take risks each day in almost everything we do. So learning to cope with risk is a vital part of our education.

A. Verdin wrote:
> Some of my extracurricular practical work came close to disaster. I attempted to emulate Davy and produce the metal sodium. The method was very simple. I electrolysed molten sodium hydroxide.

The school's electricity supply was still DC at the time, so using the full 220V carried a risk. I have often repeated the experiment as a demonstration, but using 12V batteries.

Drury's is the story I like best (J. S. Drury, MA, DPhil, C.H. 1956–63). When he was doing his VSO year in Basutoland (Lesotho now) he climbed to the upper levels of the central mountains, carrying with him a barometer to see if the atmospheric pressure really was lower up there, as he had been told. But it was not a handy aneroid barometer that he took with him, but the equipment needed to make a simple barometer – a meter-long glass tube, open at one end, a bottle of mercury, and a small dish, just as he had used in the school laboratory when experimenting with air pressure. He must have been a strange sight carrying these items up to the top of the mountain. He would have filled the tube with mercury, putting his thumb over the open end, and inverted it over a bowl of mercury resting on a flat piece of rock. He would then have removed this thumb and it must have been exciting for him to see the mercury to fall to a height of less then 76 cm, which it would have been at sea-level.

The following notes about Old Blues are extracted from the replies sent to requests for their views on the influence of C.H. science on them and their careers.

M. G. Allen, MA, BSc (C.H. 1949–57).
> After graduation from Cambridge I went into management science. I felt passionately that the management of Britain's companies needed a lot of help. Since crossing the Atlantic, I have been very lucky to have experienced a successful and challenging career in management consulting. It's hard to isolate the role of Christ's Hospital

science training in making this possible. Inductive thinking and concept creation from diverse information have been crucial skills for me. Were these pay-offs from the heuristic method?

J. D. Asteraki, MA (C.H. 1941–50).
In the course of a forty-year career in scientific research, first in the research laboratories of Marconi's Wireless Telegraph Company and then at the Royal Aircraft Establishment, Farnborough, my colleagues mostly had similar backgrounds to my own and it seemed that the teaching of science at C.H. was not out of the ordinary. However, on retirement I joined a team which visited schools to help with projects to attract students into careers in science and engineering. During the course of that activity it became abundantly clear that the teaching of science at C.H. was very far from the norm, and was, indeed, quite outstanding. My own introduction to the scientific method came in the Third Form under Miss Elizabeth Harvey, who taught biology. She was one of the then novel band of ladies who came to the rescue in the early days of the Second World War. I found her inspiring.

My start in elementary physics came in the LF under Mr Peter Matthews. He took pity on us by dictating a short note at the end of each session, which summarised what we should have learnt. Chemistry came into the syllabus in the UF when the newly recruited Mr Jarvis was the teacher. He had a wry sense of humour and instantly gained the respect of the class for his patience and his insistence that proper care was taken with the experiments and that the results were properly recorded. His untimely death was a great blow. The last of my early memories is of Miss Kate Barlow, another lady recruited during the war, who was later to become Mrs Jarvis. She taught mathematics, which Mr Harry Sills described as the queen of sciences. One lesson I remember particularly well was the class being taken onto Big Side in order to measure the height of the Big School clock with the aid of some rather primitive goniometers. An example of the heuristic method at its best and an introduction to basic civil engineering and the need to make accurate measurements.

The Manual School was where I developed the skills needed to design and make the apparatus which was so necessary in my career. I cannot speak too highly of those who struggled to impart their knowledge and skill to me. What I learnt then stood me in very good stead for the whole of my career.

M. P. Berry. MA (Oxon), MSc, Cchem, FRSC (C.H. 1949–57), chemistry teacher.
The teaching I received plus the company I kept ensured that I became an enthusiast for chemistry. My time at C.H. gave me the cast of mind and the stamina to fight consistently for a better deal for teachers and pupils, especially in the sciences in state schools. This unwillingness to sacrifice independence and integrity is probably the best gift C.H. gave me.

C. J. Bolton, MA (Oxon)PhD (Berkeley) (C.H. 1956–63).
The teaching of science at Christ's Hospital certainly influenced my choice of subject – metallurgy. There was a strong Christ's Hospital tradition in metallurgy at Oxford, where the students included Keith Bowen, John Daniel, Keith Bywater, Nick Boucher and Rick Blake. I clearly remember Dr Van Praagh introducing to us the subject of metallurgy and I later worked on a variety of metallurgical topics. I now lead the group responsible for research work in this area. I think that the heuristic teaching we had at Christ's Hospital was a good way of instilling a scientific approach.

N. A. Boucher, MA, DPhil (Oxon) (C.H. 1954–62), metallurgist.
I am sure that a knowledge of the scientific method was of great assistance to me. C.H. gave me a very good grasp of scientific thinking: the heuristic method taught me to think for myself. Rigour of thought and cogency of expression are only achieved by thinking, unprompted, from first principles. At C.H. the input into me was enormous. My teachers insisted that we thought for ourselves even at the age of thirteen.

K. Bowen, DPhil, FRS (C.H. 1951–59).
I loved *Chemistry by Discovery*[7] and I still remember my first real experience of the thrill of science when Dr Van Praagh lit a Bunsen under a beaker of water and asked us to explain the mist that immediately formed. I remember exclaiming excitedly: 'Water is gas oxide, sir!' and the joy of working it out for myself rather than being told about it. Then the high pressure crystal growth – I am still in the field of crystals in industry. With so many others I remember the freedom to enquire.

C. J. L. Buggé (C.H. 1956–63), pharmaceutical chemist.
To my mind, chemistry was magic, and I was always able to excel at it. On Sunday afternoons when the whole school in those days had to vacate the houses, Kirby's lab was where I headed, to become lost in my own experiments for three or four hours. I was always encouraged by him. His response when I had a question about a chemical reaction or 'what would happen if . . .?' would always be answered by 'Try it out, see for yourself!' These lessons served me well when I left C.H. to earn a living, eventually directing a research group working on anti-cancer drugs and others.

Professor M. R. Churchill, PhD, BSc (C.H. 1951–58), Professor of Chemistry, University of Buffalo.
I spent two years under the tutelage of Dr Van Praagh and enjoyed his enthusiasm. Chemistry by Discovery it truly was. After O level exams we had time for a research project. I distinctly remember being presented with the task of extracting gold from a section of a furnace which had been used for making purple glass. This involved the use of such reagents as concentrated hydrofluoric acid and potassium cyanide. I had two triumphs: I did obtain some gold and I did not injure or poison myself! I also learned a tremendous amount from 'Pop' Beaven. He had a different approach to chemistry and insisted upon our reading and learning from a textbook. He would have us write a paper on our previous night's reading while he carried out a complete organic synthesis on the front desk. The joy of discovering things for myself, coupled with the discipline of 'hitting the books', has served me well in a forty-year career of research in chemistry.

P. A. Cox, MA, PhD (C.H. 1956–63).
The general approach to the subject, based on the heuristic method, was certainly stimulating and strengthened my determination to be a scientist. I am sure that this experience had a large influence on my approach to science in my research, writing and teaching as a Lecturer in chemistry and Fellow of New College, Oxford.

C. Curr (C.H. 1951–59).
The heuristic approach to learning reinforced my natural way of thinking via practical discipline in the scientific method. By the 1970s I was

applying similar methods in the fishing industry, where I developed the potential of early computer spreadsheet techniques towards improving efficiency in R & D modelling. At such a point of innovative opportunity there was no alternative to the heuristic method.

Sir John Daniel, MA, DSC (C.H. 1952–61), formerly Vice-Chancellor, The Open University.
I found that the excellent general education that C.H. had given me, combined with the curiosity for the natural and technological worlds inculcated by Gordon Van Praagh, allowed me to enjoy to the full the involvement with all disciplines that is the lot of a university head (in Sudbury, Ontario). One of the lessons I have learnt in fifty years in education is that change is slow. The Open University was able to introduce distance education to the UK in the early 1970s with a big bang, but it is only today, thirty years later, that distance education is being hailed around the world as a key route to the knowledge society. In a similar way it has taken most of a century for the ideas about science teaching that inspired Christ's Hospital to become common currency. One of my most pleasurable moments was to hear Ms Wei Yu, formerly Vice-Minister of Education for China, make a speech about how to teach science to primary school children. What she said was exactly what Gordon Van Praagh was saying half a century ago. Since China has hundreds of millions of schoolchildren these ideas will influence a high proportion of the next generation of the world's scientists

J. L. Doyle, BSC, MSC (C.H. 1940–48), formerly Vice-President, Hewlett Packard.
The school was great for me because you had to do everything: cricket and calculus, physics and fives, history, rugby, house plays. For someone like me, outstanding at nothing but interested in all, it was the perfect place. As a Science Dep. at 16 the next years promised less variety so I decided to leave. My housemaster appeared not to mind, I think I had become a little too irreverent and impatient for his taste. Robert Frost characterized education as 'hanging around until you've got it' and I obviously, if wrongly, thought I had. Gordon Van Praagh has written wonderfully on the heuristic method of teaching of science at C.H., and the influence of Armstrong on the design of the Horsham

buildings to include chemistry and physics labs and the Manual School. I suspect that I have used more of what I learned there than the information three universities struggled to teach me. Apart from GVP, who was also my housemaster for a few terms, Willink, McComas (called up and killed in the war), Roberts, Edwards, Malins, Cochrane, Buck, Carey and Len Bates are all memorable among those who massively informed the rest of my life.

P. Evans, MA, DPhil (C.H. 1955–64).

I owe my career in scientific research to the teaching I received at Christ's Hospital, particularly in getting me interested in science and in how to think about problems. It definitely influenced my choice of career. The heuristic method did effectively teach us to think about what we were doing and what was happening rather than just learning facts.

P. D. Greene, MA, PhD (C.H. 1948–56).

At C.H. in the upper fourth in 1950 my morale used to undergo oscillations of large amplitude. The minima corresponded to double Greek and the maxima to double chemistry or physics. My two science teachers then, Gordon Van Praagh and Ronald Crosland, remained the mainstay of my scientific education until I reached Merton College, Oxford. Studying for the Oxbridge entrance scholarship left time for topics like the modest style of Sir Humphry Davy, the physics of music and the chemistry of titanium. I can also remember the class being told 'Every lesson is an English lesson'. Today I find young graduates laps ahead of me in the use of computers, but I am still regarded as the departmental authority on grammar and spelling.

J. B. Hooper, BSC, ARCS (C.H. 1952–1960).

My memories of the heuristic method have faded into the past but the curiosity engendered remains with me. I went into a marketing and strategic planning career when I graduated from Imperial College after C.H., and now I am consulting in communication skills to help business people improve their ability to create and deliver better communications. Clearly, application of the heuristic method is crucial to my business. Now, I am not sure I realised that almost fifty years ago in the classrooms of my old housemaster Mr Beaven, or those of VP and Ronald Crosland!

T. W. Hoskins, MA, MB, BChir, DCH, (C.H. 1940–50).
Looking back on a medical career of forty years brings home to me how strongly I was influenced by my C.H. education. In those formative years I was permanently influenced by half a dozen inspiring teachers but the major influence came from the scientists Tom Archbold and Gordon Van Praagh. They were convinced heuristic teachers from whom I learned the habit of questioning and investigating received wisdom in a mood of healthy scepticism. I had two final terms at school after gaining university entrance, and this gave me the opportunity of doing individual experimental biology under Tom Archbold's guidance and also of editing the first edition of the Christ's Hospital Science Journal, conceived by Gordon Van Praagh as a means of encouraging 'scientists' to communicate in good English. I returned to C.H. as medical officer in 1969, and the large school influenza epidemics of the 1960s gave me the opportunity of conducting a Medical Research Council trial of influenza vaccine with the support of the Guildford Public Health Laboratory. Over the course of twenty years we investigated a large number of virus diseases, and as a result C.H. has acquired a lasting place in the medical literature.

Professor A. McLean, BM, PhD, FRCPath (C.H. 1942–49), consultant toxicologist.
The list of interesting adults who taught me at C.H. is a long one, and Gordon Van Praagh is one who sticks in the memory. He once told me that my thinking about how the world works is a valuable thing to do, and can earn the respect of one's fellow thinkers. If VP taught that thinking and reading are virtues, then Bill Kirby was the personification of quick intelligence directed to practical problem solving. How can we make the tiny meat ration better? Pressure cook bones for fat, and catch rabbits! How to teach boys to do experiments? Take them to a field, give them seeds and tell them to find out for themselves, and 'Heaven help you if I catch you reading a book before you have done the experiments you have thought of'. Praise was 'Look what even the meanest of God's creatures can do'. He was self-reliance, do it, organize yourself. His sarcastic praise lives on as an encouragement. The third among a long list affectionate memories leading into science, is D. S. Roberts. His evening 'history and current affairs' discussion group was not only embedded in a conspicuously happy family life,

but led to a view of science as one among many human activities which make up society and then determine much of our private lives. It helped to strengthen my view of medicine as a part of a political structure. Epidemiology helps us to see what is important in terms of numbers in suffering and health, history tells us of the importance of individuals often versus the state.

D. Parks-Smith, MA, DPhil (Oxon) (C.H. 1948–58), ICI chemist.
It was GVP who inspired me to study chemistry. Chemistry by Discovery was a brilliant concept, but more importantly it made the subject fun and it made one work things out. I was similarly grateful to Ronald Crosland for his practical approach to physics and was lucky to have a keen chemist as junior housemaster, Denis Hutchings. All were hugely enthusiastic for science, but also GVP's 'secret' topic of trying to grow quartz crystals under pressure introduced us to the joys and frustrations of research. I owe GVP and Ronald Crosland a large debt, because they took trouble to set me on the road of enjoyment of classical music. This may be nothing to do with science, but my observation tells me that there is some underlying connection.

Professor J. Pemberton, MD, FRCP, MCFM, DPH (C.H. 1922–30), Emeritus Professor of Social and Preventive Medicine, Queen's University of Belfast.
My father was Steward of Christ's Hospital in the early 1920s and was friendly with Chas. E. Browne who came to our house occasionally, around 1923. I remember his wispy hair waving about, his kindness, his great enthusiasm for science and how he often mentioned someone called Henry Armstrong. Mr Burleigh was my chemistry master at school. He was a very quiet teacher who taught us to do all sorts of experiments. We certainly learned a lot by doing experiments ourselves. The only experience in biology I remember is when Major Green presented me and another senior boy with a goat which had died on the school farm. He told us we could dissect it. We did this and then boiled it in a large cauldron. In this way we recovered and cleaned the bones and assembled the skeleton of the goat. The effort was rewarded by a plate of us in the *Children's Newspaper*; another success for the heuristic method?

M. L. Reynolds, MA, BSC (C.H. 1949–58).
I had enjoyed messing with chemistry sets even before I went to Housie, so that when Gordon said: 'I think you should do chemistry, you'll be good at it', I followed his advice rather than that of Armistead who said 'You can do mathematics if you want to'. To my great surprise I received a Minor Scholarship to read chemistry at Wadham College, Oxford, and four years later received a 2.1 with a thesis on trivalent titanium. I think I was still coasting on the chemical thinking I learned from Gordon because I had a mental block when it came to remembering the structure of organic molecules with more than seven carbon atoms. I had fun working on titanium chemistry on Teesside but loathed the climate and was seduced by an offer from Imperial Tobacco Company in Bristol. That led to a career in the US tobacco industry and the final position of Director of Research for Brown and Williamson even though I was hard pressed to write the formula for nicotine. In retrospect my Housie experience gave me a great deal of self-confidence in tackling problems and learning new skills. These currently include improving care for the elderly as a California long-term-care Ombudsman, and assessing organisational excellence as a California Awards Senior Examiner. These are a far cry from chemistry but not from critical thinking, analysis and synthesis.

Professor W. P. Robinson, MA, DPhil (C.H. 1943–52), Professor of Psychology, Bristol University.
One feature of the kind of teaching I experienced at Christ's Hospital is that you learn to be subservient to evidence and indifferent to opinion! Subsequently I have met people with qualifications who have never done any investigations at all. All their science has been learned from a book. I have never doubted that Christ's Hospital had got it right. Everything was based on observation and experiment – we were trained to 'look' and to ask 'what' and 'why' and to solve problems. We were encouraged to use the Science Library and to think up projects. I remember being told that when we arrived at the university nobody would be organizing our studies and that we had better learn at Christ's Hospital how to do this. Later in my career, wherever I have taught, I have always adopted a problem-solving approach. I now find it somewhat depressing that the battle still has to be fought. I still have to persuade undergraduates that if they wish to become competent in

their chosen subject, developmental psychology, they need to study children: they believe the knowledge is in the journals and books.

F. J. C. Rossotti, MA, BSC, MA, DPhil, CChem, FRSC (C.H. 1938–45), Emeritus Fellow of St Edmund Hall, Oxford.

I well remember my first lesson in chemistry from Mr Burleigh: a demonstration that magnesium gains in weight when burned in a crucible. Later, we did a great deal of practical work ourselves, and there was inspirational teaching by Mrs Barber, one of our two women science teachers. Physics with Mr Sills contained large doses of the history of science. Then Ronald Crosland appeared with a more systematic approach. Nor should we forget mathematics: devoted after-supper coaching by M. B. Jones helped to launch me in late 1945 into a postmastership in chemistry at Merton, his former Oxford college. This was early in an era when C.H. was pre-eminent in the number of entrance scholarships and exhibitions gained to Oxbridge colleges. A legacy of VP's wartime experience was an interest in metals engendered in science grecians. A succession of them became my pupils as metallurgy scholars of St Edmund Hall.

D. M. Ruthven, MA, PhD, SCD, FRSC (C.H. 1950–57), Professor of Chemical Engineering.

My recollections of Housie in the 1950s are rapidly fading but some memories of VP have survived remarkably intact. My first lesson in chemistry was in September 1952. It was taught by VP and I well remember his introduction to the heuristic method. We oxidised copper by heating the metal in air and then formulated hypotheses to explain the transformation of the shiny metal to a black powder. We reviewed the historical development of ideas on chemical change – the phlogiston theory, the discovery of oxygen by Joseph Priestley, Gay-Lussac's experiment, Cannizzaro's hypothesis and the Avogadro Number. I also recall a succinct bit of advice that has served me well over the years: 'You don't need to remember all the facts; just make sure you understand the basic principles!' I remember as Science Grecians we were given a great deal of freedom to study whatever topics caught our attention or simply to browse through the journals in the Science Library. VP was always available for discussion of both scientific and more general topics but he acted as a catalyst and a resource person rather than as a traditional teacher.

M. Seakins, MA, DPhil (C.H. 1945–54). Senior Lecturer in Chemistry, University of the West Indies.

The heuristic method at C.H. with GVP seemed the most natural thing. On one occasion, four of us in the Science Deputy Grecians collaborated on a project concerning brass. One of us cast a piece of brass in the Manual School, another tested it to destruction by pulling it apart, a third boy examined the surface and the cracks with a microscope, and I analysed it by wet chemistry. The year before, everyone in our chemistry class chose one of the elements, researched that element and gave a ten or fifteen minute presentation. I chose silver and wrote off to a silver mine in Mexico, asking for a sample. Twenty-six months later back came the letter, unopened.

W. J. L. Sladen, MBE, MD, DPhil (C.H. 1930–1937), Professor Emeritus, Johns Hopkins University, Baltimore. (A distinguished naturalist, deeply involved in wildlife research in Antarctica, he made a film on the life of the Adelie penguin, founded the Wildlife trust of North America, and conducted research on teaching migration routes to geese, swans and cranes which was recorded in the Hollywood film *Fly Away Home*. He received many awards for his researches and had two mountains in Antarctica named after him. The book *The Adelie Penguin* by Dr Ainley[8] carries this dedication: 'To Bill Sladen who had one foot on the heroic side of Antarctic exploration, the other in the modern scientific side. It was his passion and thirst for knowledge that helped lead us into the modern age on Antarctic ornithology.')

My parents were responsible for my love of nature, also very much my first biology teacher, R. F .J. Brown, whom I admired tremendously. What I gained most from Housie was
(i)   The Natural History Society. I won the botany and bird prizes – and should have had the butterfly one too but was accused of cheating by catching cabbage whites and painting them!
(ii) Music from Dr Lang – I played violin in the orchestra and sang treble in the choir.
(iii) The Science Farm and the importance of sustainable farming (Why is this defunct? It should be growing food for the school and con-

ducting research in food sciences).
(iv) The Manual School. I still use the things I made there – what Latin I learnt has gone, but the things I made live on!
(v) Sport. I was good at running and later was captain of the English Universities cross-country team.

Professor D. M. R. Taplin, DSc, DPhil, MA, FIMechE (C.H. 1950–57), Professor of Mechanical Engineering, Trinity College, Dublin.
The whole approach to teaching engineering, physical sciences and metallurgy had a great impact. My entire career has continued along the lines set at Christ's Hospital in the chemistry labs and the manual school.

A. Verdin, MA, MSc (C.H. 1942–51).
I arrived at C.H. in September 1944 through a London-wide scholarship from the normal 11-year-old exam taken from my London elementary school. Later, without any clear plan, I chose engineering. This meant giving up classics for mechanical drawing in the Upper Fourth. I was tolerably good at chemistry, physics and maths and received a lot of encouragement from VP. My revelation came on a geology expedition when three of us were taken by VP to the Malverns. On the way we stopped in Oxford and looked around the grounds of Magdalen College. My immediate reaction was 'I want to come here, what do I have to do?' I was not the most reliable pupil, and some of my practical work, especially extracurricular, came close to disaster. I met Barnes Wallis with VP, and was led to see that science offered a worthwhile career and interesting opportunities. Another, not always compatible, influence was Kirby: although biology was of little interest I was a convinced Signals member.
Expert instruction in chemistry, physics and maths, and some enjoyable lessons outside (e.g. Roberts and Malins for English) won me a Postmastership to Merton College, Oxford, where I met my future tutor, Courtenay Phillips; two Old Blues, Jim Compton and Francis Rossotti were doing well and showed me the ropes. Having set me on this path, VP's direct influence faded, but the enquiring spirit and capacity to think clearly have, I think, remained with me. I enjoyed my time at Oxford in all ways, but failing to notch a first I abandoned thoughts of an academic career and worked on the border of science and engineering, for some time with small but interesting companies

and eventually for myself. Courtenay Phillips was one of the pioneers of gas chromatography, a powerful analytical technique, and as my MSc came from work in this field, my first serious jobs, with Perkin-Elmer and Mine Safety Appliances (MSA) used this background. In 1968 I left MSA and bought the Cherwell Boathouse Restaurant and Punt Station, which I still run. In 1971 I wrote *Gas Analysis Instrumentation*, a comprehensive handbook of current techniques, and started Analysis Automation Ltd, which became the leading UK supplier of analysers, especially for monitoring air pollution. In 1990 I sold the company and was left with Cherwell Boathouse and major involvement in two spin-off businesses – Morris & Verdin Ltd (wine merchants) and Chelsea Arts Club, all of which continue to keep me busy. Although I have virtually ceased to work as a scientist, the scientific method and excitement at discovery remain with me, and I try to instill this excitement in my children. I have much to thank VP for.

D. W. Willis, MA, CEng, FIEE, FBCS (C.H. 1936–45).
Although I became a science grecian, I was not taught in a class by VP. My first contact was as part of a holiday assignment for clearing hedges in the fields near Marlpost Woods in order to enlarge the fields for crops. Meals were prepared in the Scout Hall under the supervision of VP (probably cooking was regarded as a subdivision of chemistry) and since I was rather young my assignment was as a cook. One of the things I learnt from him was how to make stuffed marrow, a dish I have always enjoyed since that day. His influence in science came to me, however, through the teaching at Christ's Hospital. I have always had a scientific approach to understanding things which must, I think, derive from the heuristic teaching at C.H. Even today, if I am trying to understand a complex subject, I start by constructing a computer model as to do so demands the disciplines of understanding in detail what may be somewhat arbitrary procedures. As VP says, it is not so important what you know; the important thing is what you understand!

This may be an appropriate place to refer to the four students from different developing countries who were given places at C.H. for their sixth form work.
I had been running a course in Singapore in 1960 and was struck by the

way the schoolboys worked so hard. I suggested to the Head Master, H. L. O. Flecker, that he asked the C.H. Council to give a free sixth form place to a Chinese boy from Singapore. The boy chosen was Brian Cheow (later Chang). Brian worked extremely hard and after a year went to London University to study engineering. He went back to Singapore and had a career in the ship salvage business. Some years later I read in the *Sunday Straits Times* a half page profile which described Brian as 'typical of the up-and-coming young entrepreneurs responsible for the rapid progress of Singapore as an industrial nation'. An example of the influence of Christ's Hospital.

The second student was Mosko Reuben from Sarawak. He was selected by a small committee including an Old Blue, Ian Baillie, who was doing his VSO in Sarawak at the time. Mosko was a Bidayu – a land dayak. He was at C.H. from 1963–65 and then went to Sidney Sussex College, Cambridge, and from there to Guy's Hospital. He qualified with an MB, BS and, after staying on a year to get his MRCP, he returned to his own country, having first married in his college chapel in the presence of his ex-housemaster, Kit Aitken, and the Headmaster of his school at Kanowit in Sarawak. In the early 1980s he moved from Sarawak to Singapore where he became one of the six medical staff at Saga Heart and Lung Clinic. He rose to become the director of the clinic, which spawned two more branches in other parts of Singapore. His achievements resulted in the International Association of Heart and Lung Specialists holding their annual conference at the clinic in 1997. His elderly mother lived in a typical village house on stilts in Sarawak. In 1997 he took me to see the two-storey, four-bedroomed house he had built for her on the same site and where, at 80 years old, she was extremely, and proudly, happy.

I first came across the African boy who was to become the third student at C.H. when staying with a teacher in Dar-es-Salaam, Tanzania, in 1967. The boy's name was Sibrino Forajalla and he was a refugee from Southern Sudan. He seemed very bright and a suitable candidate for a sixth form place. At the school from 1968–71, he was very popular with boys and staff. He was at the University of Bangor from 1971–74 for his BEd and at London University from 1974–75 for his MA. By this time the war in Southern Sudan had temporarily died down and he returned to the capital, Juba, to take up a post in the Ministry of Education. He later became Professor of Education at the University in Khartoum. He married Marianna and has two sons and a daughter. In 1995 he had a book published recounting his researches in education in refugee camps. He has twice read papers at conferences in Oxford, and is now with UNESCO.

The fourth student, Nasir, was from Malaysia. He was the son of a barber (Azudin) from Malacca, and was at C.H. from 1973–76. When he saw himself listed under 'Azudin' he exclaimed 'My father is not at Christ's Hospital – it is me, Nasir!' He was a very bright boy and took part in many of the school's activities, including rugby and playing the clarinet in the band. He left for Leeds University where he got a 2nd class honours degree in food science. He returned to Malaysia as a junior university lecturer but was immediately sent back to the UK to study for a PhD as Glasgow University (1980–84). At this time he also married his childhood girlfriend, Hasnah, who was studying engineering there. His speciality was starch and his research, partly in Malaysia and for six months in Reading, led to his presenting papers on the subject at international conferences. He became Associate Professor in the university. Unusually, he set up a bakery where he made special breads and sold them to members of the staff. His reputation reached Australia where he was appointed a consultant to the Australian Wheat Board to help them solve a particular problem, namely that Australian wheat did not make good noodles so did not sell well in S.E. Asia. This led to his appointment in 1996 as research director at the Wheat Board. He moved to Melbourne with his family of six. As well as travelling widely in both Australia and S.E. Asia, he set up a pilot project for making noodles, from Australian grain of course! Sales in S.E. Asia more than doubled and he was appointed director of the Wheat Board.

Of course these were bright boys, but they all attribute their success to the influence of Christ's Hospital.

The heuristic method of H. E. Armstrong aimed at producing an understanding of science that would form a basis for those continuing their science studies after leaving school. The original heuristic method is not suitable for use under modern conditions, but the heuristic spirit has influenced the methods used in teaching science to this day, not only at Christ's Hospital. The success of science teaching projects in achieving their objective is often assessed shortly after the project is launched. But if the objectives are long term then short-term assessments are not possible. The contributions to this compilation from Old Blues form a kind of assessment of the extent to which the heuristic approach succeeds in producing scientifically minded people.

CHAPTER 4

VIEWS FROM SOME SCIENCE TEACHERS

MARTYN BERRY contacted the following who kindly contributed their views. All but Professor Jenkins are former colleagues of mine.

1. Edgar Jenkins, Emeritus Professor of Science Education Policy, Leeds University.
2. David Chaundy, Physics Teacher at Christ's Hospital 1953–1962.
3. Bryan Stokes, Head of Chemistry, King's College School, Wimbledon.
4. Terry Allsop, Director, International Research Foundation for Open Learning.
5. John Florey, Chemistry Teacher, Oundle School.

EDGAR JENKINS

In 1896, Henry Edward Armstrong was chosen by the Royal Society as its representative on the reconstituted governing body of Christ's Hospital. Both the timing of the appointment and the nominee were propitious for the future of school science education. A little over a hundred years later, what is the legacy of Armstrong, Browne and the work that was undertaken at Christ's Hospital? In an era of free mass secondary education framed by a national curriculum and burdened with assessment, it is tempting to argue that heurism, although influential at the time, is no more than an interesting footnote in the history of school science teaching and ultimately irrelevant to today's needs. The evidence is that this is far from the case.

At Christ's Hospital itself, Browne continued to teach science until his retirement in 1926 when he became science tutor at the London Day Training College, later the University of London Institute of Education. He was a seminal influence on all those whom he taught, whether pupil or student, and he helped to promote the view that any science teaching worthy of the name must allow pupils to spend at least some of their time in investigative work appropriate to their age and abilities. It was an approach to school science teaching that was sustained and developed as circumstances required by Browne's successors and their colleagues at Christ's Hospital, one of whom, Gordon van Praagh, had been a student of Browne's at the Day Training College. The record of science teaching at Christ's Hospital is an outstanding and distinctive one and it is no coincidence that it made a significant contribution to the Nuffield science teaching project of the 1960s and 1970s.

But the influence of Browne and his successors at Christ's Hospital extends far beyond the school itself. At the heart of heuristic teaching of science is a belief that no course can be satisfactory if it deals merely with the acquisition of scientific knowledge. Science teaching must also promote critical independent thought, together with reasoning and judgment upon evidence gathered from a variety of sources, including data obtained by investigation, first hand or from a demonstration, in the laboratory, workshop or field. In short, any school course in science must be permeated by a spirit of investigation if it is to be fruitful. It is this spirit of investigation that endures within school science teaching, although the manner in which it is manifest and expressed has inevitably changed with time and circumstance. The history of school science teaching is littered with obsolete expressions such as the Dalton plan, 'process science', 'discovery science' and even 'heurism' itself. Yet, if the heuristic spirit has sometimes been misunderstood, misrepresented, out of fashion or used to justify an excessive and sterile approach to teaching so-called scientific method, the central message remains untarnished and continues to animate school science teaching. School science must involve practical investigation of some sort so that pupils can gain some understanding of what it means to formulate and address a problem in a scientific manner.

The legacy is evident in the belief of secondary school science teachers that practical work in the laboratory is a *sine qua non* of their daily work, and in the commitment of primary schools to a child-centred, investigative approach to the teaching and learning of science. It is evident, too, in numerous manuals of science teaching and in contributions to the *School Science Review*, notably from 1933 to 1967 by John Bradley who taught at Christ's Hospital from 1933 to 1936 and eventually became involved in training science teachers at the University of Hull. It can also be found in several official policy documents. In 1961, HM Inspectors warned of the dangers in teaching chemistry of accepting the 'opinions of others' instead of 'taking the pains necessary to convince oneself'. Likewise, physics teaching was 'bound to entail investigation experimentally' and biology courses demanded a 'training in methods of experiment and observation'. A generation later, 'scientific enquiry' is one of the four attainment targets of the science component of the national curriculum in England and Wales, and it requires pupils to plan investigations and to obtain, present and evaluate evidence. While Armstrong would have regarded with disbelief the assessment engine that now drives school science teaching and poured upon it his distinctive brand of scorn, he would almost certainly have approved of what the commitment to 'scientific enquiry' presumably intended to achieve.

The influence of the approach to science teaching associated with Armstrong, Browne and Christ's Hospital was not confined to England and Wales. In Armstrong's own time heuristic ideas were taken up in Japan and, a century later, all contemporary world-wide attempts at school science curriculum reform take it as given that pupils must spend some time in investigative work as an integral component of their school science education. If the heuristic intention is frequently frustrated, not least where resources are scarce or even non-existent, the commitment to 'finding out' in school science remains strong. That perhaps is the enduring legacy of the work that Charles Browne and his successors promoted at Christ's Hospital.

David Chaundy

When I arrived at Christ's Hospital as a young physics teacher, I inherited the Faraday Laboratory, very appropriately named for someone whose main love was electricity. This enthusiasm was slightly dimmed when I discovered that the school's electricity was all direct current, generated in the school by generators which had been installed when the school was built. They did, however, discourage late nights, for then the small and very worn generator was used and this produced continuously fluctuating light. Fortunately the lab did have a motor generator which produced slightly variable alternating current and I soon bought another one to install in my study to run my tape recorder. Another unusual feature of the lab was the gas piping which all came down from the ceiling. This allowed the vertical pipes to be used as retort stands. The only problem was that occasional gas leaks had to be stopped with plasticine!

Faraday Laboratory was little altered since it had been built and had very generous accommodation. This included plenty of space for practical work, a classroom area, a darkroom and, above it, storage space reached by a staircase. This meant that there was no need to have rigid times for theory and for practical work. Perhaps the most striking feature of the lab was a deep trough, some two metres by half a metre with wooden sides and a tiled base, quite unlike any normal laboratory sink. This was original equipment installed so that every boy could investigate the 'monkey and rock' story. This story told of an unfortunate monkey who had a rope tied around its neck with a large stone at the other end. The monkey was then thrown into the sea to drown – but, finding that stones become lighter under water, the clever monkey picked up the stone and walked out of the sea with it. Professor Armstrong thought that investigating whether a stone really did get lighter and, if so, why, would be a good piece of physics to help introduce the heuristic method into the newly built school. Hence the need for a large trough of water with plenty of room to investigate whether rocks and other things did get lighter under water. [This trough was, sadly, removed later and not kept, as it should have been, in the C.H. Museum.]

By 1953 monkeys and rocks were no longer part of the course although we did investigate Archimedes' principle and we did try to use the heuristic method and encourage the boys to find things out rather than dictate 'facts' to them. I liked the idea and where possible I encouraged boys to work things out for themselves rather than tell them the answer straight away. I well remember handing out batteries, lamps and switches to one class and asking them to get the lamp to switch on and off. They all did it but, to my surprise, some of them had the switch across the battery so that the lamp was on when the battery wasn't being short circuited and off when it was!

I realised how much I had taken to the heuristic approach when I moved to Malvern College in 1962. There we were soon involved in designing suitable apparatus for the new Nuffield O Level course and then using it in the first trials of the course. My colleagues found it quite difficult to encourage the pupils to find out things for themselves rather than telling them everything. On the other hand I found that with the suitable apparatus and the new approach I was able to teach in a way that I had always wanted to at Christ's Hospital, but had only had limited opportunities to do so. Obviously most pupils have neither the time nor the skill to discover the whole of the physics they need for themselves, but now there are many opportunities to encourage inquiry and experiment. For me the culmination of this approach came with that part of the Nuffield A Level physics course where each pupil had to carry out a three-week investigation of any topic of their choice. Here they were on their own, with some guidance, to carry out some small piece of research and to be doing real physics rather than just learning about it.

I have always been thankful that I was fortunate enough to start my teaching career at Christ's Hospital with its enlightened approach to science teaching, the support of Gordon Van Praagh and the enthusiastic pupils.

BRYAN STOKES

The influence on science teaching of the methods developed at Christ's Hospital has been real, massive, and well documented.

Throughout the 1960s and 1970s the principle of guided discovery, of teaching science in the same way as science is practised, was taken up with enthusiasm throughout the UK and in many countries overseas which followed the UK pattern of education. In the UK this took place with the financial support of the Nuffield Foundation, and overseas, after requests from governments in S.E. Asia and East Africa, with support from the Overseas Development Administration.

It was necessary first to convince teachers that it was possible to change from a rigid examination system testing factual recall to one which could test the abilities of candidates to demonstrate those other skills which guided discovery had developed. Once the possibility of this had been realised by members of the science teaching profession the opportunity was seized – slowly at first and then in large numbers. The influence of Christ's Hospital on my own experience may be relevant.

I started my career as a science teacher at King's College School, Wimbledon, at the beginning of the 1950s. I had enjoyed enlightened and inspiring science teaching at Whitgift but, through force of circumstances, started without the benefits of a postgraduate course in education. In developing a personal style of teaching I read whatever guidance I could, and for younger pupils was especially taken with Gordon Van Praagh's book *Chemistry by Discovery*. The turning point came when I was asked to act as chairman at a training day for chemistry teachers arranged by Surrey County Education Department. Here I had the task of introducing Gordon to his audience. This was the first time that I had met him and, as it happened, the start of a life-long friendship.

Before long, the Chemistry Panel of the Science Masters Association published its ground-breaking booklet *Chemistry for Grammar Schools*.[9] The panel, which included Gordon amongst its members, was chaired by Frank Halliwell, an ardent advocate of guided discovery. It had in this booklet put together, in an authoritative manner, guidance for teaching the subject using an investigative approach. I was very impressed by this, and wrote to the Oxford and Cambridge Examinations Board asking for an O Level chemistry examination to be set for King's College School along the lines described. In their reply they told me that the booklet did not constitute a syllabus (by which was meant a list of subject contents) but if I produced a syllabus they would, for a fee of £17, set an O Level examination on it. I cleared the payment of the fee with my headmaster, wrote a syllabus, requested the style of examining, and it all came to pass. Soon afterwards I was to receive an invitation to join the Nuffield Science Teaching Project as a member of its chemistry headquarters team.

But of course, the subject content is, to a degree, irrelevant. It is not *what* is taught that is important, but *how* it is taught. The same content, and the same experiments, can be used but directed to different ends. A statement of fact by the teacher, followed by an experiment 'to show that both air and water are needed for the rusting of iron' is one way of proceeding. But how much more realistic, more science-like, to initiate a discussion of the likely causes of rusting (the iron must get wet) than to pose a question as to whether water is all that is needed; then to devise an experiment in which only iron and water are present (no air, etc.) *and then find out*.

Much of my life for the next twenty-five years was then spent, with others, in developing these ideas and presenting them in terms of viable O and A Level courses.

Terry Allsop

My first unsuspecting encounter with heurism came at an interview for a job at Christ's Hospital. I sat innocently with Gordon Van Praagh at the lunch table when he suddenly asked me 'How would you introduce the topic of water?' – not your average lunchtime conversation. And of course at that stage I had not digested the content and structure of the little red book, *Chemistry by Discovery*, by GVP.

I started teaching at C.H. in September 1963. As GVP was that year spending half of his time working on the development of the Nuffield chemistry course I was lucky enough to have a 50% timetable whilst working on experiment testing and writing for the new Nuffield course. My memories are of teaching a formidably able group of Oxbridge candidates, several of whom went on to be distinguished chemists, unlike the accountants and financial experts they might become today. In addition, using *Chemistry by Discovery* as a framework for teaching pre-O Level was simply fun.

At the end of that year, GVP left C.H. to work full time for the Nuffeld Foundation, so I took on a normal timetable for the next three years. But Nuffield had by no means done with me! Early in 1964, Gordon said to me that the Nuffield chemistry course was to be illustrated by two 16mm films, and would I consider being the teacher in one of them. So early in the summer term, the ICI Film Unit arrived to capture on film the teaching of a double lesson, malachite, to be titled *Chemistry by Investigation*. The film was made almost in *cinema verité*, with four cameras recording the whole lesson in one of the laboratories in the Old Science School. A rehearsal was run with one class in the morning, followed by live filming with a different class in the afternoon. The result was a film that showed off C.H. students at their best, being taught by a very nervous teacher. At a preview at the Nuffield Foundation offices in London, George Porter said, not realising I was in earshot, 'The only person who looks ill at ease is the teacher'.

I left C.H. in 1967 for teaching in Uganda. My expectation had been of teaching in a secondary school, but I found myself in the most interesting environment of the National Teachers College at Kyambogo just outside Kampala, under the influence of a very special head of science, John Bowles. John Florey writes on pages 41–42 of that experience, as he joined us on the staff in 1968, coming from teaching in Sarawak. Suffice to say that the challenge of helping produce the first generation of Ugandan science teachers, whilst modifying the new Nuffield chemistry course for use in East African schools, was heady stuff. So much so, that it led me to a lengthy sequence of posts in teacher education – in Uganda, Chester College of Education, Hong Kong University and Oxford University. I finally left Oxford in 1995, anxious that I should not become stale, for a senior education adviser post in ODA that took me back to sub-Saharan Africa for seven years with, however, virtually no science education responsibilities.

I have, therefore, been well placed to watch the transmission and transmutation of those heuristic ideas that stem from the little text *Chemistry by Discovery*, through their quite direct representation in the Stage 1A version of the first two years of the Nuffield Chemistry programme, to more scattered visibility in newer generations of lower secondary science courses taught in Britain and several other countries. How well have they stood up to the journey?

Well, a good many young people will heat malachite and test for the products at some stage of their school science experience, but virtually none will have an extended period of following a science course based on heuristic principles. Why not? Despite Bruner's vigorous defence of discovery learning, encapsulated in his famous dictum that '. . . intellectual activity is everywhere the same, whether at the frontier of knowledge or in a third grade classroom. The school boy *(sic)* learning physics *is* a physicist and it is easier for him to learn physics behaving like a physicist than doing something else', other factors have come to dominate over the relatively relaxed environment of C.H. chemistry in the late 1960s, where generally students were taught all of their science in classes of around twenty in number.

My assessment is that, in so many educational experiments and innovations, product testing was nothing like sufficiently intensive to generate confidence in the 'product'. In many of the early cases of curriculum innovation, including Nuffield O Level chemistry, the piloting of the new materials was carried out in atypical contexts, leading to unrealistic expectations of the average science teacher with their class of motivated and unmotivated teenagers. The extent of control and management of what goes on in schools and classrooms has increased rather spectacularly in Britain and elsewhere in the last twenty years or so. Science teachers work with a highly structured national curriculum and an equally taxing assessment regime; it is a brave spirit indeed who lingers or takes an interesting diversion. So, it comes down to the issue of who dares to innovate, to take a risk. We still know little about how much attitudes can be encouraged and then rewarded.

We should not be despondent! The evidence suggests that young people in 2003, particularly girls, when examined at GCSE or AS or A level are performing at higher and higher levels overall. What is clear is that they are tested on a different skill repertoire that generally would not be directly derived from an early heuristic experience. But if you are interested to find connections with the chain from H. E. Armstrong to C.H. science at the beginning of this century, try to access investigations done by A Level students following Nuffield Advanced Chemistry or Salter's Advanced Chemistry courses as part of the assessment profile. You would not be disappointed in regard to their investigational skills and understandings.

JOHN FLOREY (Extracts from his letter)

Christ's Hospital was my first teaching post. During my time there, from 1960 to 1964, the experience made such a deep and lasting impression upon me that throughout my teaching career I have tried to honour and propagate it. During my PGCE course at the London Institute of Education my tutor, Constance Chandler, arranged visits to a range of schools where we observed a lesson; Christ's Hospital was one of these. When I first saw Gordon Van Praagh in action I was impressed by the tight, logical sequence of his questions, and the precision of language that he strove for from his pupils. I warmed to all this immediately, as I did to the general ethos of the school. There was a post available at Christ's Hospital for the next academic year and it was my immense good fortune to be appointed to it.

I well recall my first lesson. Each pupil saw 'salt gas' fuming copiously at the mouth of their test tube. The encounter was stimulating and I was there as fellow traveller and guide. The Chemistry by Discovery course, followed up to O Level, was more than stimulating, it introduced the pupil, quite naturally, to the scientific method. What Christ's Hospital was doing was teaching science scientifically and, therefore, bringing out its moral and emotional features at the same time.

There were important foundations that were being laid in that introductory course. Sometimes in the course of a lesson pupils would suggest experiments which were set up 'on the side'. These were very small research projects, of course, but the fundamental scientific attitude was there. Another valuable feature of the introductory course was the science diary that each pupil kept. It all seemed so sensible and natural at the time. It was only some years later that I appreciated the deeper wisdom of this. 'I expected to see . . . but was surprised to find . . .' Intellect and emotion were working naturally together and the stage was set for appreciating that scientific and artistic creativity spring from the same mysterious subconscious pool.

At this stage I think I should say how I saw Christ's Hospital in the first half of the 1960s. There was a general atmosphere of quiet unassuming self-confidence and conviction. In a long teaching career I have never seen a product to rival the Science Grecians – humble, questioning, bubbling with ideas and, above all, so wonderfully alive.

During my time at Christ's Hospital the conviction grew within me that I should teach in the Third World: Gordon Van Praagh in his travels had seen that Sarawak offered exciting possibilities and December 1964 saw me married, a member of the staff of St Thomas's School, Kuching, and fired with the conviction that the scientific 'gospel' as practised at Christ's Hospital was well worth exporting. The headmaster arranged that I taught the same group both chemistry and physics in their two year run-up to the Overseas Cambridge School Certificate. The majority of the pupils were Chinese but there were also Malays, Dayaks and Indians. Initially they viewed themselves as 'vessels to be filled' rather than 'fires to be kindled', but they were amenable to being increasingly coaxed round. I returned to Sarawak in 1999 and saw a good number of this group. It was very striking that almost all were in very responsible, senior positions where 'hands-on' ability and resourcefulness were vital.

After my three years in Sarawak, I returned to England where the new Nuffield courses were taking root. Nuffield chemistry reflected, in both content and spirit, Van Praagh's considerable input. During my year in London I was in contact with R. T. Allsop, a contemporary of mine from Christ's Hospital days. He was at the National Teachers College, Kampala, Uganda. I needed no urging to respond to the exciting possibilities he outlined and I was alongside him for the beginning of 1970.

A new chemistry course was being written for the whole of East Africa (See Chapter 12). It was the English Nuffield course in spirit and in content, too, but where possible local examples were drawn in. For the pupils there were booklets of work sheets consisting of carefully graded structured questions, whilst very detailed teachers' guides were written for the teachers (plate 5). I played a major part in the writing of both the pupil sheets and the teachers' guides. Each experiment was tested meticulously and the result was a thoroughly practical course that had the stamp of scientific integrity upon it. I am sure I could not have made my contribution had it not been for my initial experience at Christ's Hospital.

A main part of my job in Uganda was to train teachers to teach this new course. I also had to teach it to Ugandan pupils at the Demonstration School which was attached to the College. My trainee teachers sat in on some of these lessons and were encouraged to comment afterwards. I welcomed this degree of exposure. Our trainee teachers responded splendidly and there was a very good working relationship.

I returned to the UK in 1973, the East Africa course essentially finished. I had experienced two years of Idi Amin's rule and things were already declining rapidly, but my decision to return was made independently of this. I then moved on to Oundle School which has a fine science tradition since the time William Sanderson was its Headmaster, 1892–1922, and I remained there for twenty-five years. I am still teaching chemistry and this year I have been assigned the task in General Studies of dealing with the contribution the scientific method has made to our lives.

CHAPTER 5

J. E. MORPURGO PUBLISHES *CHEMISTRY BY DISCOVERY*

SHORTLY AFTER WORLD WAR II, a young Old Blue had started his career in publishing. He visited Christ's Hospital one day looking for new authors. He tried to persuade me to write a textbook along the lines of our 'Guided Discovery' course in chemistry. I did not think this was practicable because the pupils were supposed to do the experimental work investigating a series of problems and find out 'what happens'. If the book told them what they would find, it would spoil the whole excitement of the voyage of discovery. However, Morpurgo suggested a way out of this dilemma – he said 'Don't describe the results of the experiment but, in the next chapter, refer to their results on the assumption that the pupils had by then, discovered them'. I tried to do this and the outcome was the production of the textbook *Chemistry by Discovery*. This was first published in 1949 by Morpurgo's Falcon Press and in 1960 by John Murray.

I did not realise at the time that this book was a milestone in the story of the spread of teaching by a modified heuristic method (which I called 'Guided Discovery') both in this country and overseas.

CHAPTER 6

'WHY DON'T YOU JUST TELL US, SIR?'

As a student at the London Day Training College, I also attended lectures by the Professor of Education, Sir Percy Nunn. He emphasised that 'a child's mind is not a vessel to be filled, but a fire to be kindled'. (It was many years before I discovered that this was not original, but a quotation from Plutarch). The heuristic method of teaching is more consistent with this philosophy than the more commonly used didactic method.

Chemistry is intriguing – one thing turns into another! It is not magic – it's a chemical reaction! How does it happen? But more intriguing, what makes it happen? Most children are full of curiosity from an early age – always asking 'Why?' They want to find out, and be told the answer. Helping them to find out is an essential part of their education. As the Education Minister of Malaysia realised (see Chapter 13), chemistry is a very suitable subject with which to use the heuristic method or the method of 'guided discovery'.

I used to start my junior chemistry lessons by giving the class a few substances to heat – chosen so that something visible would happen. I always included a piece of shiny copper foil. When heated it 'goes black'. Has it changed colour or is that black stuff on its surface? 'I can scrape it off – it must be stuff'. 'I wonder how it got there – any ideas?' Smith says: 'I think it's soot from the flame'. 'Good idea'. I write it on the board. 'Smith's theory – the black stuff is soot'. 'He may be right', I say, 'Any other ideas?' 'Yes, sir' says Robinson, 'I think it's an impurity driven out of the copper by the heat'. So Robinson's theory goes up on the board too. 'I know what it is', says Solly whose older brother is in the Fifth Form. 'If you know, you will have to prove you are right – we'll add it to our theories'. Solly's theory: 'the black stuff is formed by the air acting on the copper'. 'How shall we decide who is right?', I ask. I get them to suggest experiments to test the three theories. 'Heat it away from the air, sir'. With various classes I have heated copper foil under sand, under water, in steam, sealed in the glass of a test tube and under molten salt. Apart from the sand, all keep the air off the copper and it does not go black. 'Smith's theory must be wrong' rings out from the class. Robinson tested his theory by heating his piece of copper for a long time – he even came in after hours. But the copper never seemed to be rid of the black stuff – there was just more of it. Poor old Robinson!

We rigged up a tube from which the air could be removed by a pump so that Solly could heat his piece of copper in a vacuum and see what happened when air was absent. When it was in the vacuum, the copper, although red hot, remained bright. Then came the big moment – Solly opened the tap to admit air and immediately the colour of the copper changed to black. This experiment featured in our film *Exploring Chemistry* which will be described in Chapter 7.

Just to have answered the question 'What is the black stuff?' would have been Instruction, not Education. 'Why don't you just tell us, sir?' 'Because that would not be educating you and not teaching you to think, not helping you to understand.' Pupils trained to try to solve problems for themselves develop the skills to do so. What is more, some get keen to 'find out' and become research workers; their 'creative instinct' develops. We had lots of examples in the Science School at Christ's Hospital. So much so that we started a journal in which students could write about their researches and read about others. (See below).

FIFTIETH ANNIVERSARY OF THE TEACHING OF SCIENCE AT CHRIST'S HOSPITAL

In 1947 we celebrated the fiftieth anniversary of the teaching of science at Christ's Hospital by holding a dinner in the Science Library. Happily both Charles E. Browne and Douglas Burleigh were able to come. Afterwards Charles Browne wrote me a letter in which he said 'I thoroughly enjoyed my long weekend at Christ's Hospital, especially the visits to the Science School and the talks with masters and boys. It was evident that your weekly meetings with the staff were successful in winning their co-operation. The boys were delightfully responsive and shared a real interest in what they were doing. I never felt more proud of the Science School than I did in this visit.' (19th March 1947).

TEACHING, LEARNING AND RESEARCH

Browne's first notebook sums up his teaching: 'The teacher is to afford guidance and suggestions mainly by questioning and I shall adopt the attitude of a co-enquirer, not an authority. If the boys are to be taught anything it will be in the spirit of curiosity and this they will acquire not by formal lessons but by practical effort.' The phrase 'if the boys are to be taught anything' reminds me of remarks by a distinguished Old Blue, Dr Christopher Ounsted, Consultant Physician at the Park Hospital for Children, Oxford, who once said to me: 'Don't you teachers kid yourselves that you ever teach anybody anything – your job is to enable children to learn.' Which in turn reminds me of a quotation from the Australian writer, Patrick White: 'I dunno', said Alfred, 'I've forgotten all I was taught. I only remember what I learnt.'

In essence the heuristic method is that of the research worker and when at Christ's Hospital I became interested in the relationship between the teaching of science and research activities. Research workers are engaged in discovery – and so are the school pupils. Most children are full of curiosity and the drive to 'find out' lies behind both the idly curious and the serious research worker. Teachers should make use of children's instinct to explore and discover – for this is how they learn.

The subject of what science courses to teach and of what their content should be continues to be controversial. Some courses in General Science (under the guise of Integrated Science, Combined Science, Coordinated Science, etc.) have been introduced into many schools including Christ's Hospital. I am in no position to judge the results – so much depends on how the subject is taught. In my opinion the method of teaching is more important than the syllabus if the objective is to achieve understanding of the science. I would go so far as to say that the choice of topics for inclusion in a syllabus should be largely governed by whether or not they can be studied in an investigational manner. If they can only be taught didactically they cannot contribute much to the education of the pupil. Lecturing students does not train them in scientific methods of thinking – it only serves to load the memory with half understood and soon-to-be-forgotten facts.

Pupils studying science heuristically do simple little pieces of research. Their discoveries are not new, but they are new to them. What a pupil finds out for himself, either by direct experience or through the pages of a book, he not only remembers better but understands more clearly.

A science journal was started in 1950 so that pupils could publish some of the research they had carried out. The journal was then expanded to include articles written by pupils on a variety of scientific subjects. The first editor, T. W. Hoskins, later edited the *Cambridge University Medical Society Journal* and, when he went on to Guy's Hospital, the *Guy's Hospital Gazette*. The *Science Journal* (plate 6) was well printed and included plates and diagrams. There were special editions on the quatercentenary year (1953), and on the Exhibition of Science and Industry, etc. The authors of many of the articles later distinguished themselves in their careers, and contributions from some of them appear in Chapter 3.

Selection of Articles from the *Christ's Hospital Science Journal* 1950–64

This list of contents is intended to show the sort of articles that were contributed by boys and masters to the early numbers of the *Science Journal*.

No. 1 (1950)
i. Letter to the Editor from Chas. E. Browne:
> May I say how glad I am to hear that the Science Department is to have a magazine of its own, devoted to the interests of those who find in the study of science something more than a subject for examination? I should like to congratulate those to whose initiative and enterprise the issue of the magazine is due, and those whose sacrifice of time and energy will benefit so many.
>
> I am sure this venture would have received the hearty approval and commendation of the Founder and designer of the Science Department the late Professor H. E. Armstrong (1849–1937), one of the most famous and distinguished scientists of his day.
>
> I anticipate that the magazine will contain more than a record of observations and measurements, and will include contributions from members of the School, describing investigations carried out by themselves of some interesting problem which is to some extent original.
>
> Professor Armstrong used to say that of all the subjects in a school curriculum, practical science afforded the best training ground for practice of writing good English. Master of good English himself, he would have seen in the publication of the magazine a potential influence for encouraging the young scientist to express himself in the best possible way.

My best wishes for its success, and a long, distinguished, and useful career.
Charles E. Browne

ii.	Growing Crystals by B. G. Fisk
iii.	Ecological Survey of the Upper Lake by J. A. W. Buckley
iv.	The Chemistry of the Metal Mortuary by B. W. Palmer (An amusing article about hypothetical elements and their compounds)
v.	A Geological Expedition by J. L. Goddard
vi.	Biological Catalysis by D. J. Anderson, MSC, BDS
vii.	Visit to the Royal Society by T. W. Hoskins
viii.	Owl Pellets by P. R. Beaven (Master)
ix.	Birds' Beaks and their Uses by M. W. Woodcock

No. 2 (1951)

i.	Mining in South Africa by N. J. Miners
ii.	Tin Smelting in Malaya by J. C. Warden
iii.	Analysis of Samples from a Norwegian Copper Mine by C. N. Osmond
iv.	Perfumes, Natural and Synthetic by R. G. Harrison
v.	Aeroplane Flight by J. D. Wallis
vi.	Weather Forecasting by D. G. Linnell
vii.	Oil of Vitriol from Pyrites by R. Prowse
viii.	Visit to the Royal Society by J. K. Jones
ix.	Historic Apparatus at the Royal Institute by A. C. Falck
x.	Research laboratories of Messrs Vickers Armstrong by J. F. Duke
xi.	Badgers near Christ's Hospital by P. R. Beaven (Master)

No. 4 (1953) Quatercentenary Number

i.	Science 400 years ago by M. Seakins
ii.	The Origins of the Royal Mathematical School by T. Dee
iii.	Interview with Chas. E. Browne by J. M. Tims

No. 5 (1954) Exhibition 'Science in 1553'
This number was largely devoted to descriptions of the exhibition laid on in Faraday Workshop, including the four main exhibits on:

a.	John Dee, a 16th century alchemist (by Dr G. Van Praagh)
b.	Alchemy (by B. W. Palmer)

c. Navigation, with an exhibition of historic compasses (by G. E. P. Constable)
d. Human Biology (by M. D. Fuller)

The following noteworthy articles appeared in subsequent issues of the *Science Journal* Nos. 6–15 (1955–64):

No. 6
i. Accounts of Short Works Courses attended by boys in the holidays at the English Electric Company, the National Coal Board, Rolls Royce, Staveley Iron, and chemical companies
ii. Careers in Science – the Royal Navy
iii. Tin in Cornwall by A. H. Clark
iv. The Founding of the new school bells by M. Hughes (London Foundry, where the earlier bells had also been cast)
v. The Eclipse of the Sun, with photographs taken from the New Science School Roof

No. 8
i. Why does a Cricket Ball Spin? by J. R. Morgan
ii. Robert Hooke, famous 17th Century Scientist, Governor of C.H. and designer of the C.H. badge by J. E. Bullard, CB, BA (Master)
iii. Titanium – the metal with a bright future by T. D. Culpin

No. 10
i. The strength of England by Dr B. N. Wallis, CBE, FRS, DSC.
ii. Evolution – Centenary of *The Origin of Species*
iii. The Beginning of Metallurgy by D. L. Bowen (later FRS and Professor of Metallurgy at Warwick University)

No. 11
i. X-rays in the service of cancer by Dr L. H. Gray (Director, Cancer Research Campaign Radiobiological Institute)
ii. Quartz Synthesis by R. S. Bayliss

The contents of the last volume during my time (No. 15, 1964) included:

i. Notes and News –
Professor D. J. Anderson (Lamb B 1933–39) has been elected to a London University Chair in Physiology in relation to Dentistry at Guy's Hospital Medical School.

SCIENCE GRECIANS ENTERING HIGHER EDUCATION					
	CAMBRIDGE	OXFORD	OTHER UNIVERSITIES	OTHER COLLEGES AND TECHNICAL INSTITUTES	MEDICAL SCHOOL
1952	1	5	6	6	1
1953	3	2	3	3	0
1954	0	5	2	4	2
1955	1	5	11	4	2
1956	3	10	?	8	?
1958	4	5	1	5	?
1959	2	3	5	?	4
1960	2	5	12	3	2
1961	3	4	11	4	3
1962	2	7	9	6	3
1963	5	3	8	8	0
1968*	5	6	9+	4	1
1969*	3	1	6+	1	1
1970*	6	3	11(?)	4	0
1971*	6	2	18(?)	3	0

*Science and Maths
(?) Depending on A level results

Dr L. H. Gray, FRS (Maine B 1918–1924) has been awarded an international prize for outstanding contributions to cancer research.

The Science School has purchased much new specialised apparatus with the help of an extra £1,000 on the yearly grant from the Council. The New Science School now has a tropical fish tank, which is situated on the landing outside the Lecture Theatre. The inhabitants are flourishing and can boast a month-old addition to their number.

Mr Kirby's old laboratory, now occupied by Mr Sillett, has been partitioned so that Mr Kirby, now retired, retains about a quarter of the original space, in which he continues his many hobbies.

The School's connections with the Nuffield science teaching project have become increasingly evident during the year. In addition to Dr Van Praagh and Mr Allsop's part-time employment with the foundation, some of the project's recommendations have been tried out in the teaching of junior forms.

ii. Radioactive dating of rocks by C. J. A. Davie
iii. Time and Disorder by P. A. Cox
iv. The Investigation of Organic Reaction Mechanisms by C. Pinch
v. The Toxicity of Fluoracetamide by C. J. Bolton
vi. The use of Lead Tetraethyl as an Anti-Knock Agent by N. A. Mace
vii. Colour Television Systems by B. McCurdy
viii. A short field trip to the Malverns by F. Bray
ix. The Moon by R. Tillotson
x. Researches at Oxford by Old Blues by D. G. Parks-Smith

From No. 4 (1953) onwards, Universities and Medical Schools to which Science Grecians went after leaving C.H. were recorded. (No. 20, 1968, onwards, included Maths Grecians). See the table opposite.

LARGER RESEARCH PROJECTS AT CHRIST'S HOSPITAL

In the Science School at Christ's Hospital there was nearly always some little piece of research going on. In addition to the small projects arising out of the course work were some continuing researches undertaken by a teacher with the help of a small succession of boys. Although most boys would not be personally involved they knew that some kind of research was going on and would take a passing interest.

There were a few longer term pieces of research the results of which were eventually published. It's not appropriate to write of them in detail here, but the following is a list of their titles and the names of the journals that published them. 1. 'The reaction between potassium permanganate and oxalic acid', published in the *Journal of the Chemical Society* in 1938[10] and in a simplified form in the *School Science Review* in 1941; 2. 'Preliminary investigation of the temperatures produced in burring [teeth]', *British Dental Journal*, 1942[11]; 3. 'The Synthesis of Quartz Crystals', *Discussions of the Faraday Society*: Crystal Growth (1949) (pp. 338–341) and the *Mineralogical Society Bulletin* 1993 (pp. 7–9).

A showcase describing the work on growing crystals of quartz at Christ's Hospital is exhibited on the wall at the top of the staircase in the Old Science School.

A number of boys were involved in this research in 1961–63. One, T. Veasey, spent more time than most; he became a Senior Lecturer in

Minerals Engineering at Birmingham University. In 1995 he was seconded to the National University of Zimbabwe for two years as the inaugural UNESCO Professor of Chemical Engineering. His main task was to set up the new department with emphasis on mineral engineering.

CHAPTER 7

THE NUFFIELD SCIENCE TEACHING PROJECT

IN THE 1950S, the Science Masters Association wrote to all its members saying that their syllabus committees were considering ways of modernising the syllabus. They pointed out that pupils were still being taught that atoms were like billiard balls in structure, whereas the radio was telling kids that they were like miniature solar systems! The Science Masters Association asked for opinions and, as a result, I was put on their Chemistry Revision Committee. We met monthly on Saturday mornings, but it was soon clear that the problems involved were far too big to be tackled in this way – far more time was needed.

At this point, through the good offices of the Royal Institute of Chemistry (of which several of us were members) and of Lord Todd (Professor of Chemistry at Cambridge University) the Nuffield Foundation, of which Lord Todd was a trustee, became aware of the need for research into school science teaching. The director of the foundation, Dr Farrer Brown, was enthusiastically in favour of giving us support and the foundation agreed to provide £250,000 for this work. (In the end, they spent £1.5 million). The money was used to enable a number of experienced teachers to be released from their duties by paying the salaries of replacement teachers. Offices and secretarial facilities were also made available to us. To start the operation, a big meeting of science teachers was held at University College in Gower Street, where a strategy was drawn up. A few teachers were to constitute the research workers and to draft out some initial suggestions. These teacher-researchers, of whom I was one, constituted the headquarters teams. There were about half a dozen of us in each of the three subjects, biology, chemistry and physics.

The chemistry team (of which I was a member) was led by Frank Halliwell who, apart from having been a science teacher and a headmaster, was a knowledgeable chemist and a great enthusiast for chemistry. (Later, when the project had finished, a special chair in chemical education was created for him at the University of East Anglia.) As leader of the Nuffield Chemistry team he was supported by a consultative committee chaired by another enthusiast, Professor Sir Ronald Nyholm, Professor of Chemistry at University College, London. Nyholm was always ready to be consulted on chemical matters, but left the educational considerations to us, the teachers.

The chairman of the Physics Consultative Committee was Sir Neville Mott, Cavendish Professor of Physics at Cambridge University. In the early days of the project I was asked to go to Cambridge to answer queries about it from some of the Cavendish Laboratory physicists. The meeting was chaired by Professor Mott and questions were asked about differences the project was likely to make to the undergraduates going up to Cambridge to read physics. All welcomed a revision of school science – but for different reasons: some thought school leavers were not sufficiently well grounded in basic science, others thought they were ignorant of modern physics. I listened while they argued and eventually tried to sum up our objectives by saying: 'Although students emerging from the Nuffield courses may know less, we hope they will understand more.'

To get better understanding of scientific phenomena, the Nuffield teams believed it was very important for the students to be able to observe these phenomena for themselves. For this purpose, suitable apparatus is required. Traditional school equipment, particularly in physics, did not include items capable of demonstrating many modern phenomena. The leader of the physics team, John Lewis, therefore collaborated with a well-established firm of scientific instrument manufacturers, Messrs Philip Harris of Birmingham, in designing and producing a large number of new pieces of equipment suitable for use in schools. New apparatus for use in the teaching of biology and chemistry was also produced by a number of firms. For example, several new types of chemical balance were designed and manufactured. These were direct-reading, electronic balances and were a great advance on the old type of 'beam balance'. (For some readers these may constitute their most vivid memory of their school science – handling small weights with tweezers, and grovelling on the floor to try to retrieve those that had been dropped, must have put many pupils off the study of science).

Frank Halliwell's chemistry team started work in 1963 by considering some basic aspects of science education – objectives, methods of teaching, criteria for choosing the content of the syllabuses, etc. There were two main interconnected objectives: (i) to modernise the syllabus, and (ii) to try to ensure that science was taught for understanding, rather than merely learnt by rote. Modernising is not just a matter of adding modern topics to an existing syllabus. This makes the syllabus so full that it cannot be taught in what we considered a worthwhile way. To teach for understanding, there must be plenty of time – time for laboratory work, time for simple scientific investigations, time for discussion in the classroom. But it is not satisfactory merely to reduce the content of an existing syllabus by removing certain topics to make room for new ones. It is necessary to start building the courses almost *ab initio*, by deciding on the objectives and then choosing those topics that will best achieve them. Each topic should be scrutinised in the light of the aims of the course and excluded if it cannot justify its place. Only in this way is it possible to produce a course that is modern, worthwhile, and yet not overfull.

We decided that we would not write a textbook. Instead we thought about the different ways in which a textbook is usually used: first, as a source of basic information, second, as giving instructions for practical work, third, as a source of data and problems, and fourth, for providing some background reading. We therefore wrote a number of books, each with different functions.[12] There was *The Sample Scheme – the Basic Course*. The practical work was covered by a number of *Laboratory Investigation Sheets*, each helping the pupil to set up an experiment and guiding him through it by asking a number of questions 'What do you see happening now?' and so on. We called these 'guided investigations'. They were nearly all based on experiments from my book *Chemistry by Discovery*.

There was much discussion about the content of the 'syllabus', and we ended with a choice of two for the first stage of the course. One was largely designed by Ernest Coulson (the most experienced teacher on our team), the other closely followed the Christ's Hospital course in *Chemistry by Discovery*. The background information was provided by a number of *Background Readers*, often written by experts in the subjects. Lastly, there was a *Data Book*. This served not only as a source of data on which the teacher could set problems, but also as another source of information which the pupils could explore. It is clear that the books implied the use of a teaching method that was very different from 'chalk and talk'. So we also wrote a *Teachers' Handbook*. As we did so, we realised more and more how different the study of chemical topics at school level is from their study at university level. New teachers, fresh from college, therefore need a good deal of help, and our teachers' handbook discussed the meaning of a number of basic chemical topics at some length.

So the Nuffield teams began to build up new courses. However, courses constructed by a few teachers sitting round a table in an office may not work out well when taught in classrooms and laboratories. So a series of 'trials' was planned and carried out in a number of schools of various types. For this purpose we chose as Area Leaders in chemistry twelve teachers who collaborated with the headquarters teams in planning and organising trials of the new materials in sixty-seven 'trial schools' scattered over England and Wales. The trials extended over at least two years and feedback was used to rewrite the draft courses. After three years a number of books for both pupils and teachers were published. These were revised and rewritten about eleven years later.

New courses require new examinations. We had been a bit worried about this, but the Examination Boards were co-operative from the start. I remember an early meeting when we explained our problems to the Secretaries of all the boards. 'Don't worry', said one, 'After all, we exist to examine what you teach.' I asked him to say that again because, I said, 'Many teachers think that they exist to teach what you examine.'

During 1966–67, while the books were being prepared for publication, a 'Continuation Group' was set up to enable a wider range of teachers to become familiar with the Nuffield materials. The group consisted of one teacher in each of the three sciences, with myself as chairman. Our main task was to organise courses all over the country and in this we were greatly helped by Local Education Authorities. During that year we organised nearly a hundred courses each for about forty teachers and lasting two weeks. This involved finding suitable places in which to hold them (usually colleges or universities), finding tutors and lecturers (mostly teachers from trial schools) and handling financial and other administrative matters. To assist with these I was greatly helped by a retired accountant from Shell, Jack Mitchell. Jack was used to handling accounts totalling millions of pounds. It amused me to see him entering every postage stamp we used which, at that time, involved the expenditure of fourpence.

These courses were spread over only a few months and over 4,000 teachers must have taken part. The courses were the first contact teachers had had with the Nuffield ideas and gave them, we believed, sufficient introduction to enable them to start teaching the new courses the following term. The majority of teachers, who were not included, still wondered what 'Nuffield' was all about. Maybe our initial policy of not encouraging inquirers could have been mistaken.

Many teachers were asking exactly what we meant by the discovery method. We decided that a good means of communicating it to teachers would be by showing films of classes being taught science in this way. Among the films made were two of chemistry classes. The first was shot by the ICI Film Unit in a laboratory at Christ's Hospital, and has been described by R. T. Allsop in Chapter 4. A second film was made to give a more comprehensive view of the Nuffield chemistry course in action. Entitled *Exploring Chemistry*, it was made by the Unilever Film Unit, and gives a good idea of the way in which the Nuffield Chemistry 'sample scheme' envisaged the development of chemistry in the middle school range. It has been much used on courses for teachers and has been shown in many countries worldwide. The film was scripted in outline but the shots taken in Wandsworth School were records of spontaneous, unrehearsed episodes. One shot in particular was outstanding in conveying the excitement and delight that the discovery method can engender: Solly was doing the experiment described in Chapter 6 to see whether his theory to explain the formation of a black coating on copper when it is heated in air was correct, or whether the rival theories of his classmate could be right. It was an *experimentum crucis*. The result, clearly shown in the film, proved that Solly's theory was correct. As Solly observed the experiment he said, softly and modestly, 'My theory must be right, sir', and the broad smile that spread across his face was unforgettable. When a pupil makes what is, for him, a discovery in the laboratory, and is thrilled by it, I too experience a vicarious feeling of pleasure. These excitements are like discovering for oneself a new piece of music for the first time – they are not readily forgotten. It could be said they are a large part of what, for a teacher, makes science teaching worthwhile.

I left Christ's Hospital in 1964 to work full time on the Nuffield project, but my successors ensured that Christ's Hospital remained in the forefront of new thinking and developments. Prominent among them was Glyn James, Head of Chemistry until his retirement in 1997. He took part in the revisions of the Nuffield A level course which were published in 1984 and 1994, and co-edited the fourth edition published in 2000. He has kindly summarised for me the developments at Christ's Hospital. He writes:

> Denis Pelmore, who was Head of Science from 1964–1974, judged that it would be impossible for Christ's Hospital to do justice to the new

Nuffield Courses in some 40% of the recommended curriculum time. His team devised its own teaching programmes, based upon Nuffield material but leading to more accessible examination objectives. The first year of the chemistry course in particular still leaned heavily on Gordon Van Praagh's *Chemistry by Discovery* which included much Nuffield thinking anyway. The first two years of Nuffield Stage A was almost identical with the courses taught at Christ's Hospital.

In 1966 Christ's Hospital became one of the 16 trial schools for the Nuffield Physical Science A level development. This experience gave the Science Department an enormous injection of vitality, new ideas and new resources. Both the course and the examination were demanding, but they did allow able scientist students to study maths, biology and physical science together, leading to higher education courses in either medical, biological or physical sciences or engineering. The incorporation of a half-term individual project in the course gave opportunities for original investigations that have always been close to the heart of the heuristic tradition.

Christ's Hospital continued to offer Nuffield Physical Science until its last examination in 1988. It had always been a special course for a minority of academic schools and a minority of able students within them, but in 1970 the new Nuffield A level chemistry course was introduced alongside physical science, for the majority of sixth form pupils studying science. 1970 also saw the restructuring of the management of science in response to the increasing complexity and demand of science education. Separate heads of chemistry, physics and biology, Glyn James, Christopher Vincent-Smith and Peter Brotherton respectively, working under the Head of Science, Denis Pelmore, enabled individual departments to achieve a higher level of autonomy within a co-operative framework.

The next phase was to see a substantial re-ordering of the school curriculum which resulted in a considerable increase in the time given to science and led to the emergence of biology as an equal partner in the timetable. It was made possible by an initiative from the new Head Master, David Newsome, who set up a curriculum committee to look into the pattern of our educational provision. The building of the Arts Block which opened in 1974 enabled the two large geography rooms in the New Science School to be converted into modern biology laboratories. The committee recommended the abolition of the fast stream and the implementation of a three year course to O level in which all three sciences would be studied equally, but consume only two subjects-worth of curriculum time. An appropriate model was found in the Oxford and Cambridge Board's Combined Science Syllabus – the first 'balanced science' course anticipating the curriculum developments of the 1990s.

This was introduced in 1974. The pioneering group of independent schools involved in this initiative were attracted by the fact that pupils no longer had to make early invidious choices between the sciences that might limit opportunities later, and that all the sciences were represented without unbalancing the whole curriculum in other areas. We were not attracted by the rather traditional style of the syllabus, but adapted it to our own needs by the extensive use of Nuffield material, while using our representation on Oxford and Cambridge Board Committees to steer development in the direction we thought desirable. By this device we were able to take the best of Nuffield to enhance our courses for the able pupils and hence build a secure A level foundation while, at the same time, offering slightly less demanding courses to pupils of more modest ability. Science was also introduced into the second form as Environmental Science in which biology and geography collaborated in a new course based on the local environment. The third form course was further developed using the Nuffield Combined Science materials as a resource. These initiatives would not have been possible without the two magnificent new biology laboratories designed by Peter Brotherton, and the appointment of two new biology teachers.

Denis Pelmore retired as Head of Science in 1974 and his position was taken by Stanley Malone. There was a further reorganisation of departmental responsibilities in which the individual science departments took full responsibility for academic matters, working alongside the Head of Science, who was responsible for co-ordination and administration. During his 16 years, Stanley Malone furnished the department with video facilities and introduced and developed computing, leading to the eventual establishment of the Computer Studies Department in 1981. He re-furnished a biology laboratory, improved the Science Library and refurbished the lecture theatre as the Riches Lecture Theatre with a gift from Lady Riches as a memorial to her late husband, a former Treasurer.

The arrival of Dr Roger Hackett as Head of Physics brought fresh ideas to that department including the introduction of Nuffield A level physics, for which he was to contribute to a number of books. Dr Paul Maddren took responsibility for the development of science courses in the first two years and Christopher Vincent-Smith introduced electronics. Stanley Malone retired in 1990 and his responsibilities were assumed by Dr Paul Maddren, now called the Co-ordinator of Science.

These teachers made many contributions in the wider world. In 1968 Glyn James had published A Mechanistic Introduction to Organic Chemistry[13] and in 1985 Roger Hackett added co-authorship with Christopher Vincent-Smith of A Practical Approach to Systems Electronics[14] to his earlier publication Inquiring into Physics.[15] Christ's Hospital was following Nuffield A level courses in chemistry, physics and biology, and both Glyn James and Roger Hackett were members of the working parties which re-wrote and revised all the associated publications in the early 1980s. Other members of the department were also involved with the work of examination boards at senior levels.

In 1992 the Salter's Livery Company made a most generous gift to the school which enabled it to refurbish the laboratories in the Old Science School. The Chemistry Department was re-named the Salter's School of Chemistry, by analogy with the Royal Mathematical School, and this was opened in 1994 by Lord Porter (PRS), Master of the Salter's Company, to mark their 600th anniversary. The prestigious Salter's Prize for the Teaching of Chemistry, also initiated to celebrate the sexcentenary, was awarded to Glyn James in 1997.

Looking back years later one may ask was the Nuffield Project a success? The answer will depend on our understanding of what the objectives were. They were not to replace existing school science courses, but to use the expertise already existing among science teachers to show how these courses could be improved. We attempted to do this in chemistry by producing a 'Sample Scheme' as one way in which this could be done. Together with the Nuffield courses in biology and physics, we hoped to influence the examination syllabuses, not to replace them. This has certainly happened. Originally our idea was that the specifically 'Nuffield' courses would be phased out, but there are still many schools that teach them and take the Nuffield examinations. Perhaps this was inevitable. When the project started we spoke of 'priming the pump for change' and this we did. Subsequent changes over the years were diverse – not always along the lines the first Nuffield teams envisaged. However, there is no doubt at all that the Nuffield Science Teaching Project has greatly influenced the teaching of science, not only in this country but in other parts of the world – Africa, South East Asia, the Caribbean, and to some extent in Australia and New Zealand. In the UK the new core curriculum in chemistry in the National Curriculum is almost identical with the first two years of Nuffield chemistry, and therefore of the C.H. Chemistry by Discovery course.

In concluding this chapter, it seems to me that out of the experience of many good science teachers the Nuffield Science Teaching Project formed a kind of watershed, giving rise to the dissemination of new ideas throughout Britain and many parts of the Commonwealth. Some of the Nuffield books were translated into Italian and Japanese and maybe other languages. Later chapters will describe how they were adapted for use in many Third World countries as well.

CHAPTER 8

AUSTRALIA WANTS TO KNOW

IN 1967 when the Nuffield books were being printed and the Continuation Group were planning Nuffield courses for teachers, an Australian headmaster visited me in Mary Ward House. As a result I was invited to tour Australia and New Zealand to talk about the Nuffield Project. The Australian government would pay the fares and the hospitality was provided by the Australian Headmasters' Conference.

So in 1968 I set off on a tour of Australia and New Zealand. I was given hospitality by eleven headmasters in Australia and four in New Zealand. Several days were spent in each place and the whole tour lasted about two months. My hosts arranged meetings for me to talk about Nuffield Science with teachers and others, and also showed me around the locality. The meetings included lectures to school and university teachers, demonstrations of Nuffield experiments and discussions about teaching methods with an emphasis on discovery methods. They were held in school or university lecture rooms or laboratories. There was, however, one exception, in Canberra, where my genial and lively host, Paul McKeown, Headmaster of Canberra Grammar School, had arranged a dinner to precede my talk to members of the Australian College of Education. Never before or since have I demonstrated experiments in physics on a table only partly cleared of fine silver, glass and cutlery with bowls of fruit still circulating among the diners.

I was supposed to deal with all science subjects, but as a chemist I chose most of my examples from chemistry. However, I described the specific contribution of the Nuffield physics team as the development of many pieces of apparatus designed so that the phenomena of modern physics could be studied in school laboratories. In biology too, where traditionally the practical work had consisted largely of dissecting dogfish and earthworms and looking at bottles of pickled snakes and other specimens, Nuffield would encourage the provision of vivaria, where the life processes of living plants and animals could be studied. Biology had become what it should be – the study of Life and not, as it had tended to be, the study of Death.

Of the places I visited I particularly recall Perth. The Headmaster of Guildford Grammar School arranged an interview with Charles Court, the Minister for Industry in the Government of Western Australia. We discussed the importance of science education in the rapidly developing industries on the west coast, and I spoke of the Industrial Fund that had been set up by industries in Britain in the 1950s to help schools who needed finance to improve their science laboratories and equipment. I suggested that schools in Western Australia would undoubtedly welcome such an enterprise there too.

In Adelaide I met an old pupil from Christ's Hospital who was running a modern pathology laboratory serving both hospitals and private medical practitioners. The £1 million machine that could measure the amounts of a dozen constituents in the few drops of blood fed to it was impressive at that time. Dr Gribble and his partners had a fleet of fourteen cars that collected samples and delivered results all over Adelaide. He had been very bright at school and had clearly fulfilled his early promise. His activities provide a good example of how a good schooling in science led to an advance that was not only successful at the time but has since led to further developments that made the machine used by Gribble look 'primitive'. Gribble Pharmacies were opened elsewhere, for example, in Penang.

In flying from Perth to Adelaide I thought of the explorer Ernest Giles who opened up the land route from South Australia to the West Coast in 1875/76 after two previous attempts. (He was an old boy of Christ's Hospital). Battling against appalling conditions of drought, heat and desert, Giles drove his way through, first on horses then on camels, always plagued by flies. When he eventually returned to Adelaide he had made a round trip of over 5,000 miles and was honoured by the Royal Geographical Society. More recently, another Old Blue, C. G. Fletcher, followed in his footsteps part of the way until he found the statue erected to Giles in the desert. There is, as well, a book about Giles in the Christ's Hospital library entitled *Ernest Giles Explorer*.[16]

At Melbourne Airport I was met by my sister who was Director of the Australian Ballet until she retired in 1983. When I return to Australia, as I have several times, it is as my sister's brother. Readers may wonder what this has to do with 'Heurism World Wide'. The answer is simple: on hearing my name, most Australians were at once well-disposed towards me – I was no stranger and this friendly attitude made me feel at home and more relaxed in my discussions on discovery methods.

There were two other old friends in Melbourne, Colin Healey and Ken Mappin, both of whom had been colleagues at Christ's Hospital. As Headmaster of Scotch College, Colin Healey was much respected as a firm but kindly disciplinarian. Ken Mappin had taught chemistry at Christ's Hospital during 1951–2, and also produced the annual sixth form play. On returning to Australia he taught chemistry and produced plays at Scotch College, Melbourne. He designed and built a science lecture theatre which also served for drama productions. He did a lot to introduce Nuffield Chemistry ideas into the syllabus and textbooks of chemistry in the State of Victoria.

School science in Australia differs in its content and organisation from State to State. In New South Wales it was dominated at that time by courses written by a Canadian, Dr Messel. Although received warmly at first, the courses were shown as time went on to be too full and needed so long to complete that little time was left for discussion and practical work – the same problem that bedevils most attempts to construct 'modern' courses.

Brisbane is almost tropical: the purple-flowered jacaranda trees reminded me of Nairobi and the orchids, magnificent in their size and variety, were as fine as those of Malaysia and Singapore. I stayed with the Headmaster of the Church of England School, affectionately known as 'Churchie'. The home of Harry Roberts and his wife could have come straight out of a Victorian picture book and their life-style was, if not Victorian, Edwardian. We had steaks for breakfast and, as we sat sipping port and talking shop after dinner, Harry's wife knitted an enormous garment on outsize needles. I was glad to have the opportunity of meeting them before they retired a year or so later.

In visiting the varied schools in Australia I realised how difficult it would be for them to change their methods of teaching science. As we have found in the UK it needed a major national project (Nuffield) to tackle the problem. All I was doing was to tell them what had been involved and to take what opportunities I had to explain what was meant by the discovery method of teaching science. I would naturally discuss its advantages in teaching pupils to get a better understanding of what they were studying: unfortunately the teachers nearly all feel inhibited by the pressures of examinations.

In New Zealand I visited another ex-colleague, Reggie Hornsby, who had been a housemaster at Christ's Hospital before the War. He became

Headmaster of Christ's College, Christchurch, one of the finest schools in New Zealand, and later took on another school, St Paul's, Hamilton, raising it from near-bankruptcy to become another fine school. On visits to Christchurch and Dunedin I had informal chats about the Nuffield Project with the science teachers, usually in the laboratories or while watching rugby games! I enjoyed a trek with a school party into the Canterbury Plains. The colours of the moorlands, in particular the brilliant blue of the lakes contrasting with yellow flowers in the green meadows, were not easily forgotten. My last memory of the South Island was trying to fly up to the Cook Glacier. I was disappointed that the flight had to be cancelled because of poor weather. However, that was not the purpose for which I had gone to New Zealand!

In both Australia and New Zealand there was already a lot of interest in new ideas in science teaching, such as those coming from the USA, the *Physics School Science Course, Biology Science Course for Schools* and two courses for chemistry: *Chem. Study* and *C.B.A., the Chemical Bond Approach*. In the latter the study of chemistry began with theories of the molecular structure of substances and then proceeded to the study of the substances themselves. I recall a lecture about these courses given in Oxford by the Staff Inspector for chemistry at our Department of Education and Science, Norman Booth, at which he said of *C.B.A*: 'Personally I prefer the order A.B.C'. The director of *Chem. Study*, J. Arthur Campbell, had visited Christ's Hospital beforehand and was well acquainted with the *Chemistry by Discovery* course. That it influenced his chemistry course was self-evident.

These American courses had been produced in haste when the Russians put the first sputnik into space. They were written by American university teachers and, although they inspired curriculum reform elsewhere and were helpful to the Nuffield Project, they were only one-year courses and were not suitable for adoption in British-style school systems. Australia adapted some of the American ideas and, in particular, wrote a biology course, *The Web of Life*, which was widely used. Other Australian courses appeared, such as those of ASEP, the Australian Science Education Project, and the Wyndham Scheme in New South Wales.

These enterprises were confined to one State. In travelling from one State to another, I met a number of school and university science teachers whose interest and enthusiasm should, it seemed to me, be more widely used. I therefore put forward to the Department of Education and Science in the Government of Australia a list of names of those whom I thought would be valuable consultants in the field of school science nationwide and suggested that a group of consultants be set up for the purpose of passing on good ideas in science curricula from one State to the others. It was pleasing to hear, years later, that such a group had been convened and that at least half the names suggested had been included.

In my report I mentioned that Science Teachers Centres had recently been set up in Britain with responsibility for running in-service courses and working with practising teachers on syllabus renewal. I suggested that if a few such centres could be set up in Australia and New Zealand, they could not only carry out these tasks but their very existence would give the science teaching profession a boost and help to attract more good graduates into it. Money would be needed for such an enterprise, but with the then boom in Australian industries this might be a good time for them to help to ensure a continuing supply of scientists and engineers by investing in science teaching. After all, the school science teachers are the geese that lay industries' golden eggs!

It seemed to me that science teaching in Australia and New Zealand was encountering the same difficulties as we had faced in Britain. The problem was simply how to make school science modern and relevant and yet to allow time for students to get real understanding of the subjects. So, although it was no part of the original purpose of my visit, when I came to write my report I made the few suggestions I have described above.

I was to return to Australia in 1985 to attend a conference arranged by the International Council of Associations for Science Education. The subject was 'Science Education and the Quality of Life Worldwide'. The conference was held in the Australian National University in Canberra. Several hundred science teachers gathered; many were old friends who had worked together on Nuffield, CEDO, etc. over twenty years before.

Through all the meetings that I attended at this conference ran a thread of doubt – does science education contribute to the quality of life of the students? Of course those who study science at school in order to become doctors, engineers or agricultural scientists will eventually help to improve the quality of life for their students and others in their countries, but what does school science contribute to the lives of the rest of the students? My group, one of fifteen working at the same time, attempted to confront this question. The delegates who attended came from Sri Lanka,

Brunei, Kenya, the Philippines and three Australian states. All thought that the main objective of students and teachers was to get good marks in examinations. This dominated other objectives and as much of what was learnt was not well understood, school science contributed very little to the ordinary students' quality of life. School science should, we said, be relevant to the ordinary lives of the students and emphasise learning about diet, health, hygiene, growing better crops, land conservation, water supply and so on. These and other suitable topics, studied in a lively, practical way and tested by appropriate examinations, could lead to improvements in the quality of life of the students and their families.

But the study of science at school should, needless to say, have other objectives as well: it should give the students some idea of the scientific approach to problems, of how scientists work, of how to be curious and questioning, of how to think independently and flexibly, and of how to apply their science to real-life situations. To achieve these kinds of objectives changes are needed, not only in the content of the syllabuses, but in the methods of teaching. Of course I emphasised the 'discovery method'.

At the Canberra conference it was good to meet not only these old friends but also those from Kenya, Nigeria, Malaysia and Brunei. They encouraged me to attend the next Asian conference on science education which was to be held in Brunei in 1989. They asked me to make a contribution probably in the form of some demonstration experiments in chemistry designed to motivate students and stimulate them to want to study further. (Unfortunately I was not able to do this).

CHAPTER 9

GUIDED DISCOVERY GOES TO IRAN

'SUCH ARE THE MAZE-LIKE CHANNELS of the Persian character, and so splendidly unforeseeable the turns of Persian policy, that the political life of the country has a misty and dream-like quality.' So wrote the Middle East correspondent of *The Times* in the summer of 1961. That was the year in which I had visited Iran, ostensibly to run a course for chemistry teachers in Teheran. 'Of course you must see more of our country than Teheran', said the Ministry of Education representative at the party given, as is usual in these cases, by the British Council. 'You must go to Isfahan and see the Great Mosques, and to Shiraz to see the gardens and the tombs of the poets. And you must certainly not miss the ruins of the ancient palaces of Persepolis. Then you must see the Wandering Tribes. It is best to go by car. We will provide you with a land rover, driver and interpreter. You should allow about ten days for the trip.' 'But what about my lectures?' I said. 'Never mind about your lectures' said the man from the Ministry. In fact I managed to give my lectures *and* see Isfahan, Shiraz and Persepolis – but had to travel by air over a long weekend. Such places are unique and, in view of what has happened since, I was fortunate to be able to see them.

How prophetic *The Times* correspondent turned out to be! 'At the head of the state stands the Shah-in-Shah, successor of monarchs who ruled one of the mightiest of empires, but below him there move in a mazy motion a bewildering succession of figures and influences. Where are they now, these prime movers of a year or two ago? Some in prison, some assassinated, some gone abroad, some lonely and forgotten. . . . This is a country of latent violence and sudden fluctuations in fortune.' Since that was written the Shah has been exiled twice, Moysaddeq has been and gone, the Shah has died and religious fanaticism has taken control. But *The Times* correspondent was less happy in his choice of closing words: 'Persia has joined the West. If her internal situation remains reasonably stable and if she gets the benefit she expects from the association, she will no doubt remain with it, but it will be many years (thank goodness) before this changes the distinctive character of the country.'

One aspect of the 'distinctive character' I was to learn on the first day of my course. In the lobby of the hotel I was anxiously awaiting the Ministry car that was to take me to the school where the course was to be held. 'May I phone?' I asked the manageress. 'I am to be called for at 8 o'clock and it is already 8.20.' She laughed: 'Remember that you are in the East now!' I was to find that I had to remember this every morning and every evening – nothing happened on time. The course eventually started half a day late; the second session was cancelled because the teachers' bus hadn't turned up; the next day was a public holiday so there was no session. However, my interpreter gave a nice party in his garden that evening. We were asked for 7.30. I remembered the manageress's advice and turned up at 8 o'clock. Mr Behravesh was still in his shirt-sleeves scrubbing the tables. The guests began to arrive about 9 o'clock.

Mr Behravesh was a fine man and worked for the Allies in World War II. As a driver and interpreter he had assisted the convoys carrying Western goods through to the Russians. He was, I believe, a good interpreter, but I had no means of checking whether his long and vociferous speeches, accompanied by much arm-raising, following my simple sentences about, say, heating copper oxide, had in fact anything to do with chemistry! Being driven by him in his small car was a hair-raising experience: as he crossed against the traffic lights I said 'In our country, red means stop – green means go'. 'Yes', he said 'green means go here too, red means look before you go'. He told me 'Our people need above all two things: a firm Minister of Justice and a sense of common honesty in every person. As it is we don't honour receipts, we don't keep appointments; we have no plan, no drive. Many people live on credit; the banks hold their carpets as security. We are not stupid – in fact some of us are very clever but we are all out for ourselves; there is no co-operation, no loyalty – every man for himself – that's our trouble.' The author of the Rubaiyat of Omar Khayyam refers to:

> Those who husbanded the golden grain
> And those who flung it to the wind like rain.

The teachers on the course were all university graduates. Their knowledge of chemistry was good but entirely theoretical; faced with any practical work they were at sea, and it seemed that many of them had never handled chemicals before. The apparatus was kept in locked cupboards – it was too valuable to use! I laid on some practical exercises in the laboratory, but was advised to stay in the background at first or the students would be afraid to do anything in case they made a mess of it and would lose face in front of me. This device seemed to give them courage but when they were discussing some point with each other it sounded as if they would come to blows. I was to learn that it is quite normal for the most simple argument to be accompanied by much shouting and waving of arms.

I doubt whether my course achieved much. I was asked to write a Practical Syllabus for School Chemistry, with detailed descriptions of the experiments. The inspector, Mr New Year (Nooroozian) was to translate it into Farsi. I wonder if he ever did? One weakness of these British Council courses was that there did not seem to be any follow-up.

I cannot leave these recollections of Iran without a few memories of my visits to Teheran, Shiraz and Persepolis (plate 7). At Persepolis the ruins of the palaces of the Kings of Persia date back to the fifth century BC but now

> They say the lion and the lizard keep
> The course where Jamshyd gloried and drank deep.

The palaces were visited by Alexander the Great. Unfortunately his soldiers set fire to the dining hall, no doubt after a good dinner, so all that remains are the stone lions that surmounted the wooden pillars supporting the roof but are now fallen to the floor. The great stairways, decorated with bas-relief carvings showing the procession of visitors bringing gifts of corn, animals and other offerings to the King Xerxes III are extremely well preserved. The ruins stand out against a mountain backcloth as one approaches along a dusty desert road. The astonishing thing is that, before any of the impressive buildings were erected – the dining hall, treasury, palaces, etc. with their elaborate bas-relief carvings in stone – a vast platform was made for them, stretching for about 50 yards from the hill behind and extending parallel to it for 40 yards. The platform was made entirely of limestone blocks, about 3 ft × 2 ft × 2 ft, all fitted together with mortar but joined in places by inset tenons of iron encased in lead. It was an incredible feat of manual labour.

The ruins of the palaces, the stairways, and the beautiful carvings in the stone were being restored, and we were lucky to be shown round by the director of the site, Mr Asfah. Work was proceeding slowly, but much progress had been made since it started about the year 1900. Set into the hill behind were the tombs of some of the ancient kings of the Persian Empire, Darius, Artaxerxes, Xerxes, etc., some of whom are mentioned in the Old Testament:

> I am Xerxes the Great King, King of Kings, King of Countries with every kind of people, King of this great Earth, far and wide, son of Darius the King, the Archemenian. I made this portal of all nations. Much else that is beautiful I did. Whatever work seems beautiful, we did all by the Grace of God.

A most enjoyable and impressive visit was crowned by our good luck on the way back in seeing Bakhtari or wandering tribes, with their tents, horses and other belongings, moving alongside our route in clouds of dust.

Different, but equally exciting, were visits to Shiraz and Isfahan. At Isfahan the Palace of Shah Abbas the Great looks down over the square where, it is said, polo was invented. The magnificent mosaics, leaving a general impression of green and blue, cover the whole of the famous mosques – Juma, Shah and Lutfullah. At the end of the long *padang* is a large market, built just below ground level and consequently relatively cool. It offered attractive brassware, cotton clothing, mosaic work covering wooden boxes, and miniatures in which details were painted with a single hair. The great multi-storey bridges over the river Zaindah were crowded with people at sunset enjoying the cool of the evening. This was Isfahan; by contrast Shiraz is smaller, quieter and the home of the tombs of the poets, Sadi and Hafez. Lying below hills of yellow sandstone and sweltering in the desert heat, Shiraz provides cool havens in its gardens.

> Here with a loaf of bread beneath the bough
> A flask of wine, a book of verse and thou
> Beside me, singing in the wilderness –
> The wilderness were Paradise enow!

There are many deep green trees and shrubs, watered by the streams that appear from underground. These carry a variety of colourful fish and were indeed a refreshing sight. It was hard to drag myself away to the airport for the return flight to Teheran.

> Iran indeed is gone with all its rose
> And Jamshid's seven-ringed cup, where no-one knows
> But still the vine her ancient ruby yields
> And still a garden by the water blows.

I suppose it does – even under the present regime.

CHAPTER 10

SCHOOL SCIENCE IN SARAWAK AND SINGAPORE

'THE HEADMASTERS are waiting for you', said the British Council Representative as he met me on arrival at Kuching Airport. My plane was late and furthermore I had not been properly briefed before leaving London. 'What headmasters?' I asked, 'and what am I supposed to do?' 'You are talking to them on teaching science in the tropics', he said, 'didn't you know?' I didn't, and as I had never taught science in the tropics I was a bit worried. However, I managed to extricate myself by asking the headmasters to tell me their problems. Most of these were the problems of anyone teaching science almost anywhere, so they formed a good basis for the discussion. The headmasters were very kind and tolerant, in fact I found Sarawakians as a whole the most friendly and hospitable people I had ever met. This visit was in 1960 and I have returned to Sarawak many times since.

The native peoples of Sarawak, the Sea Dayaks (or Ibans), the Land Dayaks (Bidayuhs), Kelabits and other indigenous races, like to be called 'natives' – unlike Africans who in South Africa regard the term as derogatory. In Sarawak at that time the Chinese, Malays and Indians were immigrants and regarded as foreigners by the natives. Of course, after the federation between Malaya, Sarawak and Sabah in 1963 they all became Malaysians, but this was not so at the time of my first visit in 1960. In fact I remember being told by the wife of a prominent Chinese leader, Stephen Yong (later a federal minister) that Sarawak had petitioned the Queen not to give them independence (reminding me of the old King of Basutoland who told Queen Victoria that he was proud to be 'a bug in her blanket', although I am sure the Sarawakians would not have put it like that!). They had seen the troubles being experienced by newly independent nations and preferred to remain British. However, Britain was withdrawing from lands east of Suez and could no longer afford to keep many of her one-time colonies. Although Sarawak became part of the Federation of Malaysia soon afterwards there are still groups of Sarawakians struggling, almost certainly in vain, for independence. These groups maintain that it is contrary to the Sarawakian way of life to have to be educated in the Malay language and to belong to a Muslim state. The Dayaks are either animists or Christians and they and their children live many miles up immense rivers. To expect them to speak Malay and look to Kuala Lumpur as their capital city did not seem to make much sense. But it is happening now.

The object of my tour in 1960 was to visit schools and report to H. E. the Governor on the state of science teaching in Sarawak and to make recommendations for the future. My general impression of science teaching in Sarawak was similar to that formed elsewhere, i.e. the emphasis was on passing the examination rather than on interest in the subject itself. Most of the teachers, who were Indians, were sincere and hard-working and would have liked to make their school science more relevant to the interests and needs of their pupils, but they were held in the vicious circle of examinations syllabuses, textbooks and traditional methods. The Junior and School Certificates were not designed for those who will leave and have no further formal education, but for those who will go on. This is a common fault in the syllabuses of all countries, so obviously bad that I continue to be amazed that it is so slow to die. The tremendous emphasis on examinations is of course because the certificate is a passport to a job. In Sarawak the employers (Shell, the banks, etc.) were not altogether satisfied with their recruits from the schools, but this sort of feed-back has not had much effect on school syllabuses in Sarawak or anywhere else in the developing world.

The Director of Education in Sarawak at the time, Mr Murray Dickson, wanted me to speak out in England about the effect of this emphasis on examinations on the method of teaching and study. So on returning I went straight to see the secretary of the Cambridge Overseas Examinations Board. I said it was a waste of time and money for the British Council to send specialists in science teaching to developing countries so long as the examination syllabuses remained unsuitable and unchangeable. This was to be my view for years to come, so it was with great excitement that I found myself some years later a founder member of CREDO, (Curriculum Renewal and Educational Development Overseas): see Chapter 11. The activities of CREDO took me back to Sarawak again in 1973.

To return to my first visit: to see the schools I was taken on a fascinating tour by the British Council Representative, Peter Davis. We visited a variety of schools – in towns, in rural areas and up rivers. Several were very remote and to reach them we had to travel two or three hours in a Chinese river 'bus' up one or other of the major rivers. Rajah Brooke had been determined that the various missionaries would not compete with each other over schools, so he allotted each denomination a different river – the Catholics had the Baram, the Methodists the Rejang and the Protestants the Sarawak river. We visited all types of schools, including government and private schools, most of which were Chinese. The residential government school at Kanowit and the Dragon School outside Kuching were the show-pieces and it was exciting to see such lively work in science going on under the two enthusiastic and hard-working headmasters, one British and the other Sarawakian.

As most of the country consists of tropical jungle divided up by rivers large and small, getting to school was often a problem for pupils and teachers alike. I met a young Dayak teacher in Kapit, a town far up the Rejang River, who had to walk five miles every day along a jungle path to get to his school, often arriving soaking wet and with the prospect of another five miles to walk home afterwards (plate 8).

The Dayaks are a hard-working and intelligent people, many somewhat resembling the Chinese in their characteristics. While staying at Kanowit school as a guest of the headmaster, the Rev. Douglas Rawlins, I got to know some of the pupils individually. We arranged a number of 'pen friendships' with pupils at Christ's Hospital, and later a Land Dayak boy, Mosko Reuben, was chosen to come to the school on a scholarship awarded by Shell. I have described his subsequent distinguished career in Chapter 3. He continues to speak warmly of his education at Christ's Hospital.

The Dayaks live in 'longhouses' mostly along the river banks. A longhouse is like a small village under one roof. A row of apartments along the length of the house opens out on to a long verandah which, like a village street, is used for casual, social and formal meetings, for receiving guests and for threshing the rice. We visited one longhouse, travelling by river in a narrow boat powered by an outboard motor. After disembarking at a crude landing stage, we had to walk up a notched tree trunk to reach the verandah of the longhouse. We were most hospitably received by the inhabitants. We were asked to squat on the floor and were offered home-rolled cigarettes, and tuak – rice wine – was proffered to us by the Dayak girls in their usual dress of skirts and necklaces. The girls drink the first glass of wine themselves (to show it is wholesome) and the visitor is then expected to drain the glass offered to him: it is rude to leave any, but further glasses can be refused without contravening any custom. Later the girls and men, resplendent in their ceremonial costumes ornate with many silver disks, beads and hornbill feathers, danced for us and posed for photographs.

Hanging from the ceiling of the verandah was a net containing human heads. I was told that they were Japanese heads taken during the occupation of Sarawak in World War II. 'Head-hunting is basically a fertility rite', wrote Robert Nicol, an education officer in Sarawak and a very knowledgeable scholar. 'A party would set off for a neighbouring longhouse or village and return with a head. The head, minus the lower jaw and the eyes, was then smoked and hung up from the roof of the verandah. It was believed to ward off evil spirits.' However, as a Dayak schoolboy wrote to his pen-friend at Christ's Hospital: 'We have not practised the sport of head-hunting for many years.'

The British Council seldom spends a big fare on sending someone to a distant destination without looking at a map to see if there is a second place where they could also send him to do a job. Singapore was on the way back to England, so off I went.

Singapore

As in Sarawak it was very hot in Singapore, and humid as well. Although one frequently wanted to shower and change, there was not much point in doing so because one was soon wet through again. When I was there in 1960 Singapore was not the clean, super-efficient modern city it is now. There were still slums and beggars in the streets. The room I had in the only modern hotel was fitted with an air conditioner that flooded the floor of the room with the moisture it had extracted from the air. The high-rise buildings that have become such a feature of the city did not exist. I had several journeys outside the city and one was soon driving through jungle-lined roads. The smell of the tropics – a mixture of humid vegetation and oriental spices – was to become very familiar to me in years to come. I liked it.

I was in Singapore at the request of the British Council to conduct a course for science teachers similar to those I had run in Pakistan and Iran. The central theme was that science is much more fun for the pupils if they are meeting the phenomena at first hand in the laboratory. In Asia much of the science teaching was book-learning, but in all these countries there were key personnel who knew better: they influenced their Ministries of Education to ask the British Council to provide 'specialists' to run courses for science teachers. On these courses they were encouraged to make more use of the practical approach to science and helped to see how they could do this. Sixty to eighty teachers attended my course in Singapore. As with the population, they were mostly Chinese with a few Indians and Europeans. In addition to running the course I was asked to take part in various other activities: I discussed modern methods of teaching science on Radio Singapore; I lectured to the sixth forms of St Joseph's School on 'Materials for Modern Industry' and spoke to the Science Society of the Naval Base School on 'Atoms'.

I kept a notebook at the time and, of the many impressions formed, I recorded two in particular. The first was of the good discipline and serious attitude to their work shown by the school children. They were extremely keen to get through their examinations with flying colours and to get further education if possible. The school certificate results made headline news in the daily papers and there was keen competition between schools to get over 90%, if not 100% passes. A sad feature that year (and I'm told in other years too) was the number of suicides among pupils who failed.

The main activity of Singapore was trading: there seemed to be only limited opportunities for technically trained school-leavers, although there was scope for maintenance and repair work in the shipping, motor and radio engineering. A few industries were arising, but land was very scarce. I wrote at the time 'Unless the Federation of Malaya later admits Singapore, it is difficult to see how the island is going to cope with the 100% increase in population expected in the next fifteen years. This increase is already evident in the retention of children at school and in night schools, in the use of existing school buildings for three separate school sessions – morning, afternoon and evening – and in the over-staffing of shops by up to five-fold'. How wrong I was!

Singapore became part of Malaysia in 1963 but came out again in 1966. Since then Singapore, as an independent republic within the Commonwealth, has flourished enormously. Not only has the entrepot port greatly expanded, but many industries, including ship-building and electronic and photographic engineering, have sprung up in abundance.

The slums have gone and been replaced by high-rise flats and new land has been reclaimed from the sea. The beggars have also gone from the streets, and these are kept clean – you can be fined on the spot for throwing away bus tickets, cigarette ends, etc. Population growth has been restrained; new schools have been built and nature parks add to the hypermarkets as unfailing tourist attractions.

The second impression I recorded on my first visit concerned the shortage of good science teachers. There had been a drift away to Malaysia. To make up for the deficiency, many students at the Teacher Training College were also teaching in the schools. The science teachers who attended my course were no doubt the keenest, but they were lacking in confidence and afraid to try anything new, especially in the laboratory. As I found out later in Malaysia, their whole tradition is against discovery methods: they are there to tell the pupils what they need to know and the pupils expect just this. They regard finding out for themselves as a waste of time: 'Why don't you just tell us, sir?' For many generations school has been a place where you go to learn and to pass your examinations – and that is all: 'Confucius he say – and you jolly well learn it' – a bit unkind perhaps but not far from the truth. Students often learn by heart but do not understand and therefore cannot apply what they have learnt. That there can be something more to education than that is a thought that seemed to be only just dawning.

The Science Teachers Association in Singapore was one of the most active in any third world country and partly through their efforts a new curriculum in school science has been introduced. I was asked back to Singapore in 1969, together with a small team of British teachers to run courses on modern science. This course, we hope, helped to upgrade the teaching of science in Singapore.

During my visit in 1960, I was so impressed by the way Chinese schoolboys worked that I thought it would be good to pass on their example to the boys of Christ's Hospital. I therefore suggested to the Head Master that the school offered a scholarship to a needy, intelligent and hard-working boy from Singapore. This they did and Bryan Cheow was chosen by a small committee which included the British Council Representative. I have described his successes in Chapter 3.

CHAPTER 11

CREDO AND CEDO

WHILE WORKING for the Nuffield Science Teaching Project in 1967 I sometimes gave a lift to one of our administrative assistants. Her name was Helen Mortimer and she changed the course of my life. 'I noticed an advertisement in *The Times* this morning that might interest you', she said. It was about a new organisation to be called Curriculum Renewal and Educational Development Overseas. Helen knew that over the previous ten years I had run a number of courses overseas under the British Council. I sent for particulars and received a summons to an interview. I was faced with a board of five or six men, of whom I knew four. 'I only asked for information – I'm not applying', I said. The chairman, Brian Young, then director of the Nuffield Foundation, said that they had thought that the best way of giving me information was through an interview. That night he phoned me and offered me the job – Assistant Director (Science) – it sounded very grand! However, I had to point out that my contract with the Nuffield Foundation still had about six months to run. He said, 'We thought you could do the two jobs in parallel'. I replied that I was not very good at doing two things at once and would rather do them 'in series'. So they appointed Dennis Chisman, of the Royal Institute of Chemistry, and I joined him in CREDO six months later, where we worked, and continued to work, very happily together. We divided the world into two: he took West Africa and the Caribbean, and I took East Africa and South East Asia. The offices of CREDO were in the British Medical Association's buildings in Tavistock Square, just round the corner from Mary Ward House, home of the Nuffield Project. The director of CREDO was Robert Morris, who had been staff inspector for mathematics in the Ministry of Education: a better man under whom to work would be hard to find.

Soon after I started work with CREDO I ran a British Council course late in 1967 for chemistry teachers in Tanzania, similar to those described in earlier chapters, and a small remark sparked off CREDO's first Curriculum Development Project. After these courses the British Council usually gave a farewell party. The Chief Inspector of Education for

Tanzania, Cuthbert Tarimu, said to me 'Come back: you people come here and give us bright ideas – then you go away and we never see you again'. 'See it through', he added, wagging his finger at me. I determined then and there that I would. I went back to CREDO to tell the director about it. Robert Morris said this was the sort of opportunity CREDO had been set up to take, and that we should follow it up.

After conducting the British Council courses I always felt that, on their own, they were rather ineffective. It is no good enthusing teachers with better methods of teaching their subject unless they can be given opportunities to put the new ideas into practice. This usually meant changing syllabuses, textbooks, examinations, etc. I had always stressed this point at British Council and Ministry of Overseas Development meetings when teacher vacation courses were discussed. For these courses to have much effect, the local Ministry of Education must co-operate in, or at least be sympathetic towards, the idea of a full-scale curriculum development project. This involves reviewing and probably revising the syllabuses, both for teaching and for the examinations, writing suitable books for pupils and guides for teachers, and providing them with re-training courses. This was just what CREDO had been set up to do – on a government to government basis. So here was a chance, in East Africa, to start our first Curriculum Development Project.

It became known as EASSP – East African School Science Project. One feature of special interest was that it was a regional project involving all three of the countries of East Africa – Kenya, Tanzania and Uganda. Apart from the postal system and the railways, it was about the only regional activity left in the region at the time! It is of interest also because it involved many local teachers as well as expatriate British teachers. Their collaborative work led, after six or seven years, to the publication of new school science courses, pupils' books, teachers' guides and other books at minimum cost: see Chapter 12.

CREDO handled many other projects, mostly in science and mathematics. The biggest Curriculum Development Projects with which I was involved were EASSP and the Secondary Science Project in Malaysia. As a result of the latter project, all aspects of secondary school science in Malaysia were affected – the syllabuses in biology, chemistry and physics, the textbooks, the examinations and teacher training, both pre- and in-service. After about ten years all secondary schools had changed to the so-called 'Modern Science for Malaysia': see Chapter 13.

About three years after it began CREDO was merged with two other organisations concerned with education overseas: OVAC, the Overseas Visual Aids Centre, and CETO, the Centre for Educational Television Overseas. All were sponsored by the Nuffield Foundation and the Ministry of Overseas Development. The new organisation was called CEDO – Centre for Educational Development Overseas. I used to say that CREDO (I believe) was a venture of faith and CEDO (I give up) gradually handed over our projects to local personnel. It eventually ceded its remaining activities to the British Council in 1974 and in a few years time disappeared altogether. Most people have not even heard of CREDO or CEDO – rather sad because we did a good job together and influenced the teaching of science and mathematics in many third world countries.

Robert Morris, as Director of CREDO, visited many countries overseas doing what he picturesquely described as 'ventriloquising requests' from them for help from CREDO. As a result we were asked to collaborate with many countries in tackling their educational problems. These were usually concerned with making their school syllabuses more suitable for their present-day circumstances. Two of our big curriculum development projects are described in subsequent chapters, but there were many small projects with which CREDO and later CEDO was able to help in a number of ways such as giving advice, initiating changes, supplying financial support and, in a few cases, providing full-time staff.

There were three other CEDO projects in which I was involved, and there were of course many others with which I was not concerned. During the Malaysian Science Project there were occasions when I visited nearby countries, Thailand and Indonesia. A third was Hong Kong. Here we responded to the request of the Hong Kong Government to run some 'familiarisation courses' about Nuffield Science. There was so much talent among science teachers in Hong Kong that it was only necessary to plant a seed for it to bear fruit.

Another project was in the Seychelles. These sunny islands, with their beautiful bays and beaches, their hills and coconut plantations, and their superb fishing and boating activities, are not ideal for new ideas in science education! The few schools were simple, poorly equipped and short of teachers. Any improvements in hand had been started by a few local enthusiasts supported by two or three 'experts' from Britain. The schools were so few, small and scattered in the countryside that it seemed to me they were a good example of schools that could make more use of radio lessons and films. When CREDO merged with OVAC and CETO there was the facility to make more use of visual aids, films and television in our Curriculum Development Projects. The Seychelles seemed a very appropriate place in which to do this. I brought the 'experts' together for a couple of meetings to discuss the possibilities, but nothing much came of the idea, partly because of lack of personnel and other resources and partly, I believe, because in that country the climate is not conducive to making efforts to do much outside the established routine. Perhaps my recollections are jaundiced by the fact that, while being rowed in a small glass-bottomed boat to view and photograph the coral in the sea bottom, I felt so appallingly sea-sick that I couldn't care less whether or not I ever saw the Seychelles again!

1 H. L. O. Flecker and his Head of Science, A. R. Quraishi

2 *Professor Henry E. Armstrong*

3 *Charles E. Browne. 'The right man to take charge of the Science School'*

4 *Quraishi introduced me to staff and pupils (in their ceremonial turbans) at Aichison College, Lahore, as coming from 'the world famous Science School of Christ's Hospital'*

5 (above) Collage of E.A.S.S.P. books

6 (left) Cover of the Science Journal

7 The ruins of the palaces of the Kings of Persia dating back to the 5th century BC

8 Walking to school from a kampong

9 *The Law of the Lever. A student in Zambia wonders how a small weight can lift a heavier one*

10 Tan Sri Dato (Dr) Haji Hamdan, Director General of Education, Malaysia, 1969

11 The British tutors and Malaysian teachers in a Curriculum Development Course in Malaysia

12 *My team of tutors for the Malaysian Project*

13 *Science teachers attending a Malaysia Curriculum Development Course*

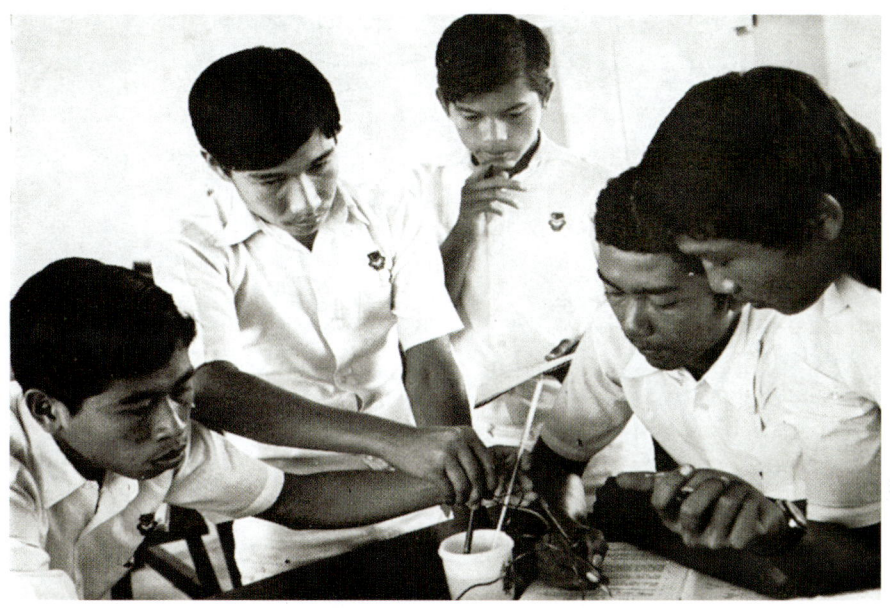
14 From the film *Learning Science in Malaysia*

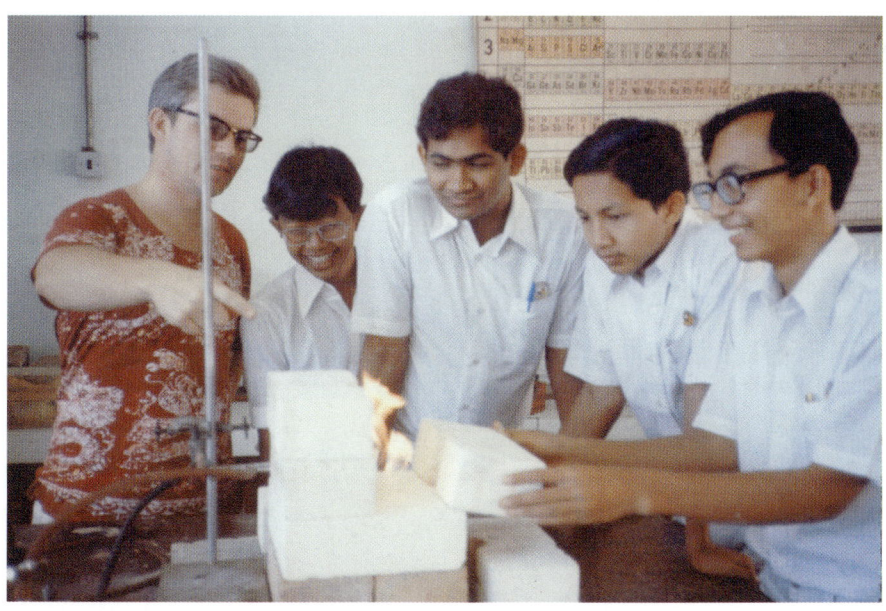
15 'Chemistry by Discovery' in Malaysia

16 *The Chief Minister visiting the School Science Exhibition*

17 *Teaching chemistry as I did half a century ago*

CHAPTER 12

CREDO'S FIRST CURRICULUM DEVELOPMENT PROJECT – EAST AFRICA

'SEE IT THROUGH', said the Tanzanian Chief Inspector of Education at the conclusion of a Teacher Vacation Course I had been running in Dar es Salaam. The East African School Science Project was a direct result of Cuthbert Tarimu's remark. He perceived that one-off courses need a follow-up. The British Council used to organise such courses for British science teachers working overseas. The science being taught in East Africa, and in most of the other countries mentioned in earlier chapters, was based on the Cambridge Overseas School Certificate syllabus which had remained almost unchanged for many years. The British Council courses were intended to give teachers some new and modern ideas to act as a stimulus to them in their routine work. But it is of little use to give teachers new ideas about the teaching of science if the circumstances under which they teach do not enable them to put these ideas into practice. Changes in the examination syllabuses, textbooks and re-training courses for teachers are needed, in other words what is known as a full-scale Curriculum Development Project.

The Inspector stated that some of his teachers had already started working together to produce a new school science for Tanzania. This was in 1966. In 1967 Cuthbert Tarimu asked CREDO to help in starting a curriculum development project and in seeing it through to the end. Thus CREDO's first science project was born. The course I had been running was intended to familiarise teachers with the Nuffield Science ideas and was held under the auspices of the British Council. In July and August of the following year, 1967, similar courses were running in Kenya, Uganda and Zambia. When CREDO was asked by these countries for assistance, we offered it in the form of co-ordination of activities and finance. It fell to me to co-ordinate the Project; so started a series of journeys and visits in East and Central Africa. There were preliminary discussions, in particular with the Chief Education officer for Kenya, Mr Mwendwa, a lively, Western-educated man. Robert Morris, the director of CREDO, had already visited him and he had accepted the idea that CREDO might be able to help by sponsoring a curriculum development project.

THE NAIROBI CONFERENCE

It was agreed that CREDO should organise a conference to discuss how to get the project started. The idea was conveyed to Tanzania and Uganda and the Ministries of Education in the three countries were pleased with this suggestion. A two-day conference was held soon afterwards in Nairobi, in March 1968. It was attended by the Chief Education Officer for Kenya and the Chief Inspectors from Uganda and Tanzania, together with representatives of the institutions where the curriculum development was already beginning, leading teachers from the three countries, and representatives from Zambia, Malawi, the British Council and CREDO. Robert Morris took the chair, with Mr Mwendwa from the host country sitting on his right.

Robert Morris pointed out the unique features of the proposed project, namely (i) that it was not confined to one country but was a regional project; (ii) that the work of writing new courses in the three sciences would be undertaken by a great variety of teachers and teacher-trainers in all three countries; and (iii) that the extra funding involved would not be great because no-one was being seconded from his paid employment.

To open the conference I read a summary of the activities in East Africa that had led to the Project. I remember feeling very happy that my views on the need for a full-scale Curriculum Development Project were at last being put into practice. The desirability of a regional project in which teachers from all three countries should participate was discussed. Mr Mwendwa pointed out that developments up till then had been largely the result of enthusiastic individual effort, but that future collaboration would require the more general involvement of a wider range of educationists in all three countries.

Mr Tarimu drew attention to the efforts being made in Tanzania towards 'education for self-reliance'. President Nyerere's book of that title had recently been published and Mr Tarimu thought that science taught in the new manner would help in realising this goal. Mr Mwendwa welcomed the emphasis in the new science course on the method of enquiry and on the involvement of pupils and thought that if these schemes would develop the right attitudes in both pupils and teachers they would constitute an exciting advance in education in East Africa. The success of the project would now depend on the collaborative efforts of all concerned. So far, the writing had been done by expatriates; now it was hoped to involve more African teachers so that they could gain the experience that would be needed for the longer-term development of science education in Africa.

As CREDO's co-ordinator for EASSP, one of my continuing activities in Nairobi was to visit many 'trial schools'. The courses seemed to have been pitched at about the right level for most pupils to understand and enjoy. Laboratory investigation sheets had been written to help pupils pursue 'guided discovery' in their practical work. The way of using this was not always understood by the teacher; in one laboratory class I watched the girls extracting the colouring matter from bougainvillea leaves. They were grinding them with a little alcohol using a pestle and mortar according to their laboratory work-sheet. This was intended to guide them through the experiment without much help from the teacher. I commented to one girl: 'You've got a nice deep colour there – why don't you go on to the next step?' She replied: 'We have to keep grinding until teacher tells us to stop.' When I pointed out to the teacher that she should let the girls proceed at their own pace, she said: 'If I did that, some would finish before others and then what could they do?' So the teacher needed a guide-book too, and these were subsequently written.

Teachers taking part met regularly, to exchange ideas and plan the next lessons. Organising and financing these meetings, with teachers travelling long distances between States, had its problem but this was where CREDO was able to help. Visits to schools in outlying areas were particularly useful. For example, I found when I visited Mombassa, on the coast, that the teachers felt 'out of it' – communications with Nairobi were poor. So we suggested that they form a local branch of the Kenya Science Teachers Association and also ask the British Council to hold their next teacher vacation course in Mombassa rather than Nairobi. At the other end of Kenya, at Kisumu on Lake Victoria, the teachers were anxious to be involved in the project. So we arranged for all the trial materials written by the panels to be displayed in the British Council office in Kisumu – teachers could study them there and send any comments they had back to the panels in Nairobi.

Eventually a number of books were written by leading members of the team and included for each of the four years of the courses: laboratory investigations sheets, teacher resource books, background readers and books of questions (plate 5). Copies of theses are all kept by John Florey who, together with about six other East Africa teachers, was responsible for writing them (See Chapter 4).

The Kampala Conference

Halfway through the Science Project we held another conference, this time in Uganda. Peter Davis, the British Council Science Officer for Uganda, organised this second regional conference. It took place in May 1970 and lasted three days. At this halfway stage much of the material for the first three years of the courses had been written in draft form and the first two years' work had been tried out in about 120 schools. The burden of typing, duplicating and distributing the books fell on a small number of people, mostly from the Institutes of Education, the universities and the British Council. Future work of this kind was among the many practical topics discussed at the Kampala Conference.

The writers and teachers on the East African subject panels kept in close touch with the three Ministries of Education and were fortunate in getting the co-operation of key personnel. In fact the project was, in its own way, a remarkable exercise in collaboration between the British Council, providing the services of several of its officers in the field; CEDO, providing finance and co-ordination; UNESCO, assisting where personnel were available; and the three ministries, without whose co-operation through their inspectors and the staffs of their schools the Project could not have got off the ground and the courses, when written, could not have been adopted in the schools. One inspector of chemistry, John Steward, was an old pupil of mine from Christ's Hospital. He did sterling work for the project, including writing some chemistry textbooks.

At the conclusion of the conference plans for the future were drawn up in detail by the subject panels. The Ministries had become more aware of the work being done, and the writers and teachers had learnt more of how their jobs fitted in with the Project as a whole. So, in addition to the work of planning, the conference also brought about an increase in mutual understanding.

Opinions began to be expressed concerning the 'success' of the Project. It was too soon for a formal assessment to be made, but the following comments were of interest.

On Independence Day in Kenya, the Minister of Education wrote in the press that the new secondary school science courses, whose development was nearing completion, were more relevant and suited to the needs of the country than the existing courses. Once finished, the new courses would be extended to a greater number of schools. A preliminary evaluation of the physics course concluded: 'SSP Physics is undoubtedly suitable for East Africa. Pupils are gaining more understanding of their physics.' Of the biology it was said: 'The findings of this preliminary evaluation are encouraging. The overall success of the course is demonstrated by its acceptability in the schools and by its relevance to life after school – as seen by the pupils'. Informal comments by teachers of the chemistry course included remarks such as 'Children enjoy, understand and remember their chemistry much better than before'.

School Certificate examinations were held in November 1971 and 1972, the total number of candidates being 1,200 and 2,600 respectively. The Curriculum Development Project had satisfactorily completed its trial period by 1973. Books for pupils and teachers for Forms 1–4 had been written, tried out in a number of schools and re-written in the light of these trials.

At first Malawi and Zambia had not been involved with EASSP. To find out whether they would like to take part in some way, I visited both countries.

In Lusaka Professor Yates in the Faculty of Education in the University had a small group of enthusiastic teachers around him. Together with the Ministry's science inspector, we held short courses in which we examined the Nuffield materials with a view to adapting them. One episode stands out in my memory. I was watching a class carrying out a fairly well known experiment in physics – 'to verify the Law of the Lever'. What made it unusual to me was that a Zambian boy, aged about 14, asked me a question about the experiment that I had never been asked in the UK (plate 9). He said 'How can a small force at the end of the lever exert such a big force near the pivot?' 'Because', I said, 'the small force is much further from the pivot than the big one'. 'I know', he said, 'but why should that make it more powerful?' He was really thinking about what he was doing – not merely carrying out practical instructions and trying to get a good result. I fear that this is usually the very limited objective of most pupils doing practical science.

In Malawi, the British Council's science officer, Stan Moss, and the

Professor of Chemistry, Professor Leiston, and others were working to improve the standard of science teaching. They held several meetings for me with teachers, inspectors and the local examinations secretary. We visited Zomba, where the new capital of Malawi was now situated. The Science Centre there formed a lively focus for science teachers' activities. It supplied new ideas and provided opportunities for discussion and for trying out practical work. At the university chemistry teaching had been influenced by methods recently adopted by McQuarie University, Australia. There were no lectures – each student had a programme involving reading, laboratory work and project work, through all of which he was guided by his tutor. This was proving a more effective use of time and staff. Lectures may seem economical in terms of staff time, but how ineffective they can be!

I met Professor Leiston again a year later when he chaired a conference on the teaching of chemistry in Africa held in the University of Nairobi. He was well ahead of his colleagues in his thinking about education in chemistry. There is no doubt that he and others in Malawi provided lively stimuli for the teaching of science in that country. They were able to produce their own school courses and get them accepted by the examination board. Taking part in EASSP was not possible for them, again because of shortage of manpower.

Unfortunately later events in East Africa put a halt to the adoption of the new courses. In Tanzania a diplomatic row caused all expatriate teachers and other civil servants to leave the country in mid-1968. Their ministry later decided to construct a hotch-potch course out of the traditional and modern courses, so the effectiveness of EASSP was much reduced. The advent of Idi Amin in Uganda led to the massacre of several Ugandans who had taken part in the project, including a leading headmaster who was also a scientist and a keen supporter of EASSP. When the next regime took over the country the modern science courses began to appear again in some schools. The only one of the three countries in which EASSP continued to develop was Kenya. Several new textbooks were written by local teachers and published by Heinemann. Later the courses spread to more schools.

Was EASSP a success? The objectives of producing new school science courses suited to East African schools had been achieved. Whether the details of the courses were followed or not, the Project had injected new life into science teaching in East Africa. It had enabled these newly independent countries to move smoothly from the traditional courses of the Cambridge Overseas School Certificate to a school science they had themselves played a key role in constructing,

An outsider's view of EASSP appeared in a UNESCO publication *Teaching School Chemistry*.

> Another well known regional project came to be known as the School Science Project in the East African countries of Kenya, Uganda and the United Republic of Tanzania. The initial driving force for reform came not so much from an external agency but from science teachers in these countries whose interest had been aroused by the recent publication of curriculum innovations in other countries. A British organisation then known as the Centre for Curriculum Renewal and Educational Development Overseas (CREDO) was asked to help, and G. Van Praagh ran courses for chemistry teachers in all three countries. A conference was held in Nairobi in 1968.... The need for new science curricula and for more appropriate examinations was discussed, and it was agreed that the three ministries of education would work together in producing new four-year courses in biology, chemistry and physics. The aim was to develop modern courses relevant to the needs of the countries which would stress understanding rather than rote learning. The courses would contain much practical work and involve an investigational approach to science teaching.

CHAPTER 13

'SCIENCE BY DISCOVERY' THROUGHOUT MALAYSIA

WHEN THE BRITISH were in Malaya before independence in 1957 they established a number of secondary schools for the most promising pupils, and left village primary education to the local people, the Bumiputra. The Tamils working in the plantations ran their own primary schools, and the Chinese ran both primary and secondary schools for their children. Thus big differences existed between the schooling of the three races, Malay, Chinese and Indian. Bumiputra or 'sons of the soil', mostly Malay in race, make up about fifty-two per cent of the population of Malaysia, the majority of the remainder being Chinese, with about ten per cent Indians. The Chinese were the most highly educated and, although they had come into the country two or three centuries ago as poor peasants looking for a new life, they had greatly prospered. Work in the tin mines had provided some with considerable wealth and they had started up many successful commercial enterprises. Their schools were well funded. Many school leavers were sent to universities overseas and those that remained had no difficulty in finding jobs. They worked hard, made more money and, living mostly in the towns, established themselves as leading citizens of Malaya. The Malays were left way behind educationally.

So at the independence of Malaysia the new government had difficult problems to solve, particularly in the field of education. Plans were in hand for some time before to advance the education of the Bumiputra but, as some educated Malays realised, the pace was too slow. A 'grand plan' was therefore evolved by the new government, included in the National Economic Plan, and put into practice during the years following Independence.

A key figure behind the 'grand plan' to advance the education of the Bumiputra was Datuk Haji Hamdan bin Sheikh Tahir, Director General of Education in the 1960s and until 1977 (plate 10). Later, as Tan Sri Haji Hamdan, he became Vice-Chancellor of the University in Penang from 1978 to 1982. Hamdan had vision, a friendly personality, the ability to get on well with people and an excellent memory for names. He was a very hard worker and a first class organiser. The ministry, and later the university, were fortunate to have such a man at the top. And of course he was a Malay. He was naturally concerned to advance the education of the Malays both for their own sake and to enable them to play a more dominant role in their own country in education, in business and in government, areas where Chinese and Indians continued to predominate.

The Ministry of Education, led by the wise Minister, Datuk Hussein Onn (later to become Prime Minister) wanted school science to be the medium through which pupils would be weaned away from authoritarian teaching, which tended to make them accept whatever they were told, towards methods leading to understanding, the development of creativity and the ability to apply what was learnt in everyday life. He expressed the view that the best subject through which students could be educated to think logically and to understand what they were learning was science. (In case my readers suspect – perish the thought – that I have dreamt this, I should say that I had the privilege of sitting next to the Minister at a lunch and he talked to me at length about this matter and others.) His Ministry, led by Hamdan, had the task of implementing these ideas.

In 1967 Haji Hamdan visited CREDO to discuss educational developments in Malaysia. At the time of the visit CREDO was involved in organising our Secondary Science Project in East Africa. Hamdan wanted something similar in Malaysia, and it fell to my lot to initiate and look after the Malaysian project. I was very happy about this, as I had enjoyed my previous visits to Malaysia under the British Council.

I have described our Malaysian Secondary Science Curriculum Development Project in my book *Seeing it Through*.[17] Rather than quoting that here, I will quote the references to the Project made in Hamdan's biography.[18] I hope this will give readers a better idea of how fully committed Hamdan was to the use of discovery methods and will justify the assumptions implied in the sub-title of this book:

Modern Science and Mathematics for Malaysians: A Revolution in Teaching and Learning

> Another aspect of national education policy which commanded Hamdan's attention was the problem of Malay weakness in science and mathematics. ... Hamdan, for one, did not believe that weakness in

science and mathematics was an inborn Malay trait, nor that Malays could not be trained to become competent doctors and engineers, etc. if given the proper opportunity. He was convinced that it was all a question of approach, or of how these subjects were taught....

Hamdan gave much thought about the ways and means by which students, especially Malay ones, could be encouraged and motivated to take up science. One obvious necessity was to multiply the number of effective Malay science and mathematics teachers, but this by itself would be insufficient. Equally important was to introduce a new approach to the teaching and learning of these subjects, particularly in science. Hamdan became a convert to the concept of the 'discovery method' of learning, that is, learning through observation and enquiry, supplemented by practical experiments conducted both inside and outside the classroom (plate 15).... In short, the discovery approach represented the practical application of basic scientific method to classroom learning. It also represented a stimulating replacement of the prevailing mode in Malaysian schools which was very much content-based and teacher centred with practical work largely confined to demonstrations by the teacher.

Hamdan was instrumental in introducing four programmes involving the teaching of science and mathematics.... The actual planning had begun with a small unit in the Ministry of Education.... Since no change in the actual syllabus was involved, their job was focused on designing techniques which would assist in re-orientating classroom teaching to the 'discovery method'. This involved providing the teachers with guides and workbooks, together with guidelines on how to improvise simple equipment from local materials for conducting experiments, and instructions as to how to adapt classroom arrangements....

By the end of 1970 it had become obvious that the Special Project was becoming a great success, and with Hamdan's direct encouragement the scheme [pioneered initially in specially selected schools] was extended to all primary schools in the country, urban as well as rural, Chinese and Tamil as well as Malay and English. To enforce this programme lecturers selected from the 25 teacher training colleges in the country at the time were briefed on the discovery approach at the Science Centre in Kuala Lumpur prior to the courses for key personnel being held. In this way, teachers sent to the schools to launch the project would have been exposed to both the rationale as well as to the practical application of science and maths learning by discovery.

INTEGRATED & NUFFIELD SCIENCE AND MODERN MATHS: THE REVOLUTION AT SECONDARY LEVEL

While the introduction of the discovery method was being essayed at primary level, Hamdan also saw to it that complementary programmes were being put in place at secondary level. The first two of these, the Integrated Science and Modern Mathematics programmes, were introduced on a trial basis in 1969. Then, in 1972, they were supplemented with the introduction of the Nuffield Science programme for the furtherance of the discovery approach to upper secondary school levels....

The discovery method for secondary level was based on British models. Given the long connection between Britain and Malaysia in education, particularly with regard to the examination system, Hamdan's own personal experience of the British system of education, and the fact that sweeping reforms in science education were taking place in that country at the time, it was quite natural that on seeking to implement this new approach in Malaysian schools he should turn to the British for guidance.

For this purpose Hamdan and a group of his staff made a special journey to Britain in 1967. Hamdan was particularly interested in visiting CREDO, a newly established organisation for promoting the latest British curricula and teaching methods overseas. It was at the CREDO headquarters that he met Gordon Van Praagh, its Assistant Director (Science), a pioneer in the development of the discovery approach in Britain.

An end-note inserted at this point reminds us that 'Perhaps the first textbook based on the discovery approach ever to be written was produced by Dr Van Praagh at the instance of a publisher friend of his. Titled *Chemistry by Discovery* it was first published in 1949. Incidentally, the Nuffield Science Teaching Project, based on the discovery method, was launched in Britain in 1963. In this way he became involved from the early 1960s in the Nuffield Science Project, which led to his becoming a global traveller pushing his wares. But of the eighteen countries where he operated he liked Malaysia best.'

A major curriculum development project developed. Under agreements reached between the Ministry of Education and CREDO the details of the implementation of a ten year programme for establishing a completely reformed system for the teaching of Science and Maths in Malaysian secondary schools was devised. There were to be three main stages. The first consisted of exposure courses led by British teams of teachers organised by CREDO (plate 12) for the Malaysian teachers who would be implementing the new system in their respective schools (plate 13). The next stage was for writing sessions to produce course materials for the students and guides for the teachers. These sessions were to be under the supervision of British teachers, but the actual writing teams would be made up of both British and Malaysian teachers. The third stage was that of implementation, a process started on a trial basis at certain selected schools and gradually expanded as other schools acquired the necessary trained staff and equipment. It was also to be accompanied by in-service courses for key personnel which would provide opportunities for feedback as to progress made and the introduction of modifications if thought desirable. The British end of the operation was to be led by . . . Dr Van Praagh for the adapted Nuffield courses. At the Malaysian end the whole operation was made the responsibility of the Ministry's Schools Division under its head, Kum Boo (now Dato') . . .

By 1972 those who had embarked on the Integrated Science and Modern Maths courses in Form One were now ready to enter on the Nuffield Science and Modern Maths courses in Form Four. . . . In the meantime a discovery approach adaptation, called Modern General Science, of the General Science Course for the Arts Stream was also created along similar lines and introduced in 1974. Therefore, by 1976 the first cycle of innovations from primary to upper secondary (Form Five) had been completed. By the early 1980s, the discovery approach to the teaching and learning of science and mathematics was being carried out in all Malaysian primary and secondary schools. . . .

Gordon Van Praagh relates in his reminiscences how initially his team consisted, besides himself, of two British Biology, Chemistry and Physics teachers who visited Malaysia each year for eight years (i.e. 1969–76), sometimes twice in one year, for periods of from four to six weeks (plate 11). Pupils' books and teachers' guides for all three pure science subjects in forms four and five were then re-written based on feedback from the trial schools, first in English, then translated into Malay and published. 'The publishers', continues Dr Van Praagh, 'worked hard for us – to produce these twenty-four books to a deadline was quite an achievement. Robert Morris, Director of CREDO, had asked me "How are you going to get all these books written?" Well, it was done . . . by many people, British and Malaysian, working hard, often in their spare time.'

This was not the end of the story. Quite apart from actually creating the course material and putting it across to Malaysian teachers, the relevant Cambridge examination papers had to be revamped to fit in with the new approach, temporary foreign teachers had to be recruited until there were sufficient numbers of Malaysian science teachers available, and new schools built to cater, in particular, for the rural areas.

By any standard, the conversion of science and maths teaching in Malaysia from the old to the new was a remarkable achievement. All those involved were in no doubt that the driving force behind its implementation was one particular man, Hamdan.

The next chapter in the biography deals honestly with some of Hamdan's difficulties:

> A problem which Hamdan found more difficult to overcome was negative reactions amongst a good number of parents and students alike to the implementation of the new approaches to the teaching of science and mathematics. . . . With such a large-scale exercise, there were bound to be shortcomings and inadequacies – sometimes unsuitable locations, sometimes inadequate funds, sometimes the problem of trained teachers who had not mastered the content of their training.
>
> More basic and harder to rectify was the general attitude shared by teachers, parents and students alike that it was the examinations that mattered, and that established teaching methods (including rote learning) were reliable and should not be interfered with. . . . Despite all the efforts, planning and strategies which were essayed, Malay students continued to lag far behind in the fields of science and mathematics, and right up till his last day at the Ministry Hamdan never ceased to exhort both parents and pupils to change their mind-sets, overcome

their lack of self-confidence, and take full advantage of the facilities and opportunities to progress that the Government (through the Ministry) was offering them.

In my book *Seeing it Through* I explained that new examinations were needed, so courses were run for examiners in the Malaysian Examinations Syndicate, who were later to take over the examinations from the Cambridge Overseas Examination Board. On a visit to a girls' school during the trials, I was surrounded by a critical crowd of fifth formers. 'You are using us as guinea-pigs, you are trying out your new courses on us and we shall suffer in our exams.' I tried to explain to them that the examiners also knew that they were guinea-pigs and would treat them sympathetically: 'You may even do better than you otherwise might!' This comforted them – but they were right. On returning to the UK, I visited the Cambridge Overseas Examination Board to explain the situation to them. They agreed to set the pass mark so that as many examinees would pass in each school as had, on average, over the previous three years. This seemed fair enough and I hope the girls agreed.

Before a school could change over to the new courses, approval had to be given by the Ministry. This would depend on whether the school had adequate laboratories, equipment and teachers. By the 1980s, all schools in peninsular Malaysia had changed to the Modern Science. To help teachers to understand the new courses and how they should be taught we made a film entitled *Learning Science in Malaysia* (plate 14). As with the films made for Nuffield Science in England, this was to be *cinema vérité*. We filmed in six schools that had taken part in the trials and chose teachers who seemed to me to have 'got the message'. We were anxious that they should not rehearse the lesson beforehand, so I waited until one day before the film crew were due to visit them before breaking the news to each teacher that he (or she) was going to be filmed taking a class. All were rather shocked at the sudden news. I tried to comfort them by saying that this way they would only suffer one sleepless night!

The film was shot by the National Broadcasting Training Centre and lessons in all the science subjects being taught at various levels were filmed. Sometimes the camera was focused on the teacher, sometimes on the class, either taking part in a discussion or doing practical work in a laboratory or in the field. Ten reels of film were shot and sent back to England to be edited. CEDO chose a very experienced editor. She shut herself away in a small room with her reels of film and a monitor, and, subsisting on cigarettes and sandwiches, she created out of the ten reels one reel that linked various extracts together to form a continuous story. I then wrote the commentary, which was also translated into Malay. When training teachers later in the university, I showed the film many times and it always provided the basis for a good discussion.

Certain memories of the Project remain vividly in my mind. I am haunted by the vision of the school laboratory assistant who, when asked to provide us with a certain chemical, would invariably reply 'No have'. In fact schools were quite well supplied with chemicals and equipment, but the laboratory staff did not always know what was in the store. Then there is the memory of about thirty teachers in a great variety of costumes, Indian ladies in colourful saris, Chinese men in neat white shirts and a few shy Malays, all trying to do experiments in the laboratory that they had never performed before, sometimes with unexpected if not disastrous results. The experienced traditional teachers on our writing sessions seldom wanted to change anything. They would say 'the students need it for their examinations'. They found it difficult to believe that anything as sacred as examination syllabuses could be changed!

During the trial period I recall having a snack with a few fourth-form boys. I asked them what sort of science they were studying at their school? 'We do something called Nuffield', said one. 'You sound as if you don't like it', I said, 'why not?' I have since often quoted his reply. 'Well, we're supposed to *understand* it – there isn't enough to *memorise*.' This reply typifies the attitude to education in so many parts of the world – it is a question of learning a whole lot of material by heart, whether understood or not, and reproducing it in the examination. This is what educational reformers are up against – centuries of rote learning.

TEACHING PRACTICE

The periods of teaching practice are, in my opinion, the most important part of teacher training. One advantage of the four year combined course, as run by the University in Penang, was that it was possible to have three periods of teaching practice. To visit students during these times was one of the duties of lecturers in the education faculty. In order to find a sufficient number of schools in which students could do their teaching practice we had to go far afield – many miles from Penang. This enabled me to visit schools in many parts of Malaysia. Some schools were over seventy miles away and we might have to spend the night in a government resthouse at the nearest town.

I think I was the first lecturer to fail a student on his teaching practice. 'It just isn't done.' But I had six students whom I would be ashamed to recommend to any Headmaster for a job. Anyway, there is no stimulus to improvement better than the occasional failure. As a result I had to take these six students for an extra two weeks' training, pointing out to them in what way they needed to improve if they were to pass. It was partly a question of their making themselves heard so I found myself giving 'voice production' lessons. Their other weakness was inadequate preparation of the lesson beforehand, especially for practical classes. Said one student: 'I've told the lab assistant what to put out'. He hadn't done it and chaos resulted.

School Science Exhibitions

In visiting schools in Malaysia (and some other countries) I saw a great deal of enthusiasm among both pupils and teachers for their science lessons. The best evidence for this was the way they organised school science exhibitions. These took place in several locations, but the only one I saw was in Penang. Every year almost all the secondary schools put on a display of exhibits of projects in chemistry, biology and physics. There must have been nearly a hundred displays of various kinds, ranging from working models and active chemical reactions to simple diagrams and posters. Teachers were greatly heartened by the fact that each year the exhibition was visited by the Chief Minister of Penang, Dato Lim Cheong Yiew (later Tan Sri). His knowledge of science was considerable and he spent much time in questioning the pupils about their exhibits . . . and sometimes telling them a bit more about their subjects than they knew themselves (plate 16).

In 1978 Hamdan became Vice Chancellor of the University in Penang. My contract as senior lecturer there had almost ended but Hamdan said: 'You must not go just as I come', so I stayed another two years.

CHAPTER 14

IMPROVISED LABORATORIES FOR CHEMISTRY BY DISCOVERY

TO LAY A GOOD FOUNDATION and understanding of elementary chemistry by using the discovery approach does not need an elaborate laboratory or complicated apparatus. However, practical work of some kind is essential if investigations into chemical phenomena are to be made. This seems fairly obvious but two young teachers recently wrote an article in *Education in Science*, the house magazine of the Association for Science Education, entitled Practicals have Gone. I replied as follows:[19]

> Practicals have *not* gone. The enormous advantage that science teachers have over teachers of most other subjects is that they can bring their pupils face-to-face with the subject matter. I need only quote the London pupil who, when asked to draw an island, drew a concrete slab with a lamppost in the middle. That is what happens when the pupils haven't the faintest idea what the teacher is talking about.
>
> Work in the laboratory should be at the heart of science teaching not an optional extra. We are supposed to be letting our pupils experience what science is about – to appreciate what is meant by scientific investigation – to observe phenomena, to speculate about possible explanations or theories, to devise experiments to test them, and to decide which theory best fits the facts.
>
> *Work in the laboratory is an essential and indispensable part of worthwhile science education.*

When I arrived at the Centre for Educational Studies (CES) in the University in Penang (USM) I found that there was no laboratory for the use of the centre. We had to use those of the chemistry, physics and biology departments, a very unsuitable arrangement. However, there was a large unused Nissen hut next to the CES and it was suggested that I should adapt that for our use. It was large enough to be partitioned into two, each side being suitable for a laboratory of about twenty students.

A laboratory needs water supplies, sinks, low voltage electricity outputs and sources of heat. In our Nissen hut there was one water tap, one sink, two mains electric points and no source of heat. For the latter, we used camping gas burners – excellent substitute for Bunsen burners. There was a shelf at about head level extending all around the walls. On this we placed very large bottles of water with a plastic tube acting as a syphon and a spring clip as a tap. Buckets are better than sinks – they don't get blocked up! For low voltage electrical supply we had to buy a fairly expensive converter to plug into the one socket and fit distribution wires around the room. We used flat movable tables both as peninsular benches around the walls and, when moved into the centre of the room, as classroom desks facing the blackboard. Very simple, but the labs were in constant use for science teaching method classes.

I have always regarded the weeks of 'teaching practice' as the most important part of teacher training. At USM we had two periods of about four weeks when students were attached to a school and became 'student teachers'. It was quite a problem to find enough schools for them; to do so we had to go far and wide outside Penang, into other towns and rural areas. I remember one school in particular that was situated inside a rubber plantation several miles outside a small town. Here the ingenuity of the teacher was fully stretched and their 'improvised laboratory' was very ingenious. There was a water supply, so that was not a problem. For heating camping gas burners could be used, but the school was too poor to afford a voltage converter, so they had come up with the following alternative: they bought three car batteries, 6–12 volts, one was in use, a second was at the town garage, being charged, and the third was in a teacher's car either on its way to be charged or to the school to be used!

The sort of apparatus and chemicals needed is quite simple. We are only thinking of the first two or three years of a chemistry course (such as is described in my book *Chemistry by Discovery*.) The need is really only for test tubes, glass tubing, burners, low voltage batteries, a few metals, carbon, sulphur and a few oxides and other compounds. It's surprising how much chemistry can be investigated with this (but don't forget a box of matches!)

CHAPTER 15

THE NITTY GRITTY

AFTER EACH OF MY VISITS OVERSEAS, I made a Report: this would be to the British Council after a 'Specialist Tour' and to the Governing Board of CEDO following visits concerned with a Curriculum Development Project. These reports provided much of the information used in the previous chapters. The British Council tours were one-off jobs. What use was made of my reports on them, I have no idea – except that the report made after my first visit (to Pakistan) seems to have resulted in my being asked to make a second tour. Maybe this continued to be the case because when the then Director of the British Council, Sir Paul Sinker, retired he wrote to me to tell me that I had made more Specialist Tours than anyone else! Be that as it may, there was a sense in which these tours led to my being involved in CEDO.

The CEDO Reports were rather different. Not only did they give an account of a visit, they made suggestions for further visits and requests for support in various ways. Copies of many of these reports exist. I have chosen a short one to conclude this chapter so that readers can get some idea of the nitty gritty that lay behind the execution of a project. This report is just one of many that were concerned with the Malaysian Project (Chapter 13).

When I think back over these years I am astonished at the load of responsibility that we in CEDO had borne! I do not remember feeling this at the time. Considering the expenditure and the demands on many people's time and movements that were at stake I should have been far more nervous than I was! Of course the responsibilities did not lie only on my shoulders; several colleagues were also involved.

The Malaysian Project, in retrospect, seemed to have resembled a living organism: if one branch or limb failed, the whole Project would nevertheless continue to grow, powered by its 'heart' which lay in the Malaysian Ministry of Education. The East African Project seemed different, partly because it involved three different nations. It was more like a collection of loosely connected small machines – if one failed, the other carried on independently.

The objective in both Projects was, of course, to produce new school science courses with pupils' books, teachers' guides, appropriate examinations and many other accessory materials. In Malaysia this happened in a planned continuous manner and seemed to be self-generating. All the books were published by Longmans in Malaysia: special courses were run for examiners, etc. Progress in East Africa was more uneven: several groups among the teachers involved wrote various textbooks and teachers' guides which were published by Heinemann.

EASSP only continues to be used in certain areas, whereas 'Modern Science for Malaysia', modified a little by their own Curriculum Development Centre, is still, I believe, the course used in most secondary schools in Malaysia.

An Example of a CEDO Report

To: Director General, CEDO
CONFIDENTIAL

REPORT ON VISIT TO MALAYSIA
February 27 to March 21, 1972, by Dr G. Van Praagh

The object of this visit was three-fold:

(i) To visit trial schools now teaching "Modern Science for Malaysia"
(ii) To plan the summer courses for the Malaysian Project with the Ministry of Education
(iii) To attend the second annual conference of Senior National Administrators at RECSAM (Regional Centre for Science and Mathematics)

1. Trials of the 4th year work in Modern Science for Upper Secondary Schools.

1.1 The 4th year courses in Biology, Chemistry and Physics, written over the last 2 years, are now being taught in about 26 schools. These include English and Malay medium schools and are distributed over the country from Johori Bahru to Kangar in the West and from Kuantan to Kota Bharu in the East. Through arrangements kindly made by the Ministry and the British Council, I was able to visit 17 of these schools. The journeys were made mostly by car, accompanied by Mr M. P. Prabhakar, of the Ministry, Mr K. Bromfield, British Council, (on one journey) and Mr Tan Teik Kee, State Science Supervisor for Penang, on the visits in his State. In Ipoh, I was accompanied by Mr O. Pereira, State Science Supervisor for Perak. In all, about 1,400 miles were covered. The schools visited are listed in an Appendix [not included here].

1.2 The visits enabled us to discuss with Headmasters, Senior Science Teachers and the Science staffs of the schools, the various problems they are meeting in teaching the new courses. We also watched lessons in progress and spoke with the children while they were working in the laboratories. Much information was obtained which will be useful when the time comes to re-write the books. The following were the main points to emerge:

(i) <u>The Pupils</u> are very much more lively and interested than those studying in the traditional way. The books seemed to be at about the right level, although in the Malay medium schools, some simplification may be desirable.

It was interesting to be told that pupils who had studied Integrated Science, rather than the old general science, were more at home with the laboratory work but that there did not seem to be much difference in their ability to understand and discuss the work.

There is a need for Readers in Chemistry and Physics in addition to the pupils' workbooks. Such Readers are in preparation.

There is also a need for reference books. Some modern School Certificate books are available in English medium schools, but there is an urgent need for suitable books to be translated into Behasa Malaysia as soon as possible. Some titles were suggested to the Ministry for immediate translation by the Dewan Behasa.

(ii) <u>The Teachers</u> varied in the extent to which they seemed to understand the desired method of teaching. Some graduates were doing excellent work, others were still 'lecturing'; some non-graduates were also working very hard in preparation and some very good lessons were seen. A few non-graduates were finding it a bit of a struggle and had not sufficient confidence to teach in the new way. With no text-book to teach, it was impossible for them to teach in the old way either. It is therefore very important to give them full support through the Teachers' Guides. These should give considerably more detailed guidance to the teacher on how to conduct each lesson. The Chemistry and Physics Guides are particularly deficient in this respect. They should dwell more on the preliminary discussion preceding each topic in order to make clear the aims of the topic, and should include an introduction on Objectives and Syllabuses.

NB: There is a shortage of science teachers, particularly in the Malay-medium schools. Movement of teachers from school to school has made the trials ineffective in certain schools, and these have had to revert to the traditional science courses.

(iii) <u>The Books</u>. As mentioned above, a number of additions and improvements are needed. It was interesting to note that the Workbooks were used in different ways by different schools. On the whole, pupils preferred to write notes in the books themselves on the blank sides of each page. There is no doubt that this procedure makes for lively work and ease of revision.

However, it is costly, and it may be necessary to produce the books with no blank spaces. In this case, pupils will have to make their notes in separate notebooks. The economic use of the books by passing them, or selling them to other pupils, is also a consideration.

(iv) <u>Apparatus</u>. Almost all schools (but not quite all!) complained of the cost of buying the equipment and of delays in supply. Some schools had raised money on their own initiative, others were spreading the expenditure over several years and gradually building up their stocks of apparatus. Delays in supply were already up to 6 months. I undertook to try to ease this situation by seeing that suppliers in the UK and their agents in Malaysia knew what equipment is needed for the 4th–5th year work, and how many schools will be involved during the coming years.

(v) <u>Miscellaneous Notes</u>

(a) In one school, the science staff met weekly for discussion and had prepared a questionnaire for the children who had changed from traditional to new type science. There were some lively and amusing answers, and it was interesting to note the high percentage that were in favour of the new courses and the reasons given.

(b) A request was made for a collection of questions at School Certificate level for use in preparation for Examinations.

(c) There is a need for more Laboratory Assistants and a new scheme is in preparation by the Ministry. It was suggested that a course for Laboratory Technicians should be held and a request from the Ministry to the British Council for such a course may be on the way.

(vi) <u>Feedback</u>. The need for modification of the draft material is being assessed in three ways:

a) By visits such as were made in this tour.

b) By means of 'feed-back forms' which are being sent to all trial schools by the Ministry, to be returned, filled in by the teachers after each topic in the course has been completed.

c) By getting the teachers together for thorough discussions. This will happen during the July/August courses this year.

2. Plans for current year, 1972.

2.1 The draft Teachers' Guides and Pupils' Workbooks in 5th year Biology, Chemistry and Physics are at present being printed by Longmans of Malaysia. They will be used in the trial schools during 1973 and will also be needed for the preparation courses for teachers in July/August of this year. These courses will be held in Kuala Lumpur from Monday 24 July to Friday 4 August (2 weeks).

2.2 The teachers who will attend the courses should be those who are teaching the 4th year work and who will teach the 5th year work in 1973. Also included should be a few new teachers who may find themselves teaching 5th year in trial schools. It is also desirable that Heads of Science or Senior Science Teachers should attend so that they can give understanding support to their staff.

2.3 These courses will be followed by a 10-day workshop, starting on Monday 7 August to continue the development of the course in Modern Science which is to form a one-subject course for the Arts streams. Much preliminary work has already been done by the Ministry and it will be the task of the workshop to build on this and write drafts for a Pupils' Book and Teachers' Guide. These could be discussed with teachers in 1973 and should be ready to teach, in trial schools in 1974. The workshop will end on 16 August.

2.4 It is hoped that a meeting in the Ministry to survey progress can be arranged for Saturday morning, 12 August.

2.5 It is also hoped that visits to schools for three tutors can be arranged for 17–20 August. Schools in Kuala Lumpur could be visited on 17–18 August; on the 19th the tutors could fly to Kota Bharu and see schools there on the 20th. Mr Yaha Ibrahim would arrange this.

2.6 Meanwhile, three other tutors will go, as requested by the Directors of Education of Sarawak and Sabah, to Kuching and Kota Kinabalu to discuss the draft guides and their suitability for East Malaysia. This visit, of a few days only, will help to determine to what extent modifications or alternatives would be needed in order to make the courses developed in West Malaysia also suitable for use in Sarawak and Sabah.

No further requests to CEDO for financial support will be necessary at present, as this is already covered by CEDO 32.

April 1972

CHAPTER 16

CENTENARY DAY AT CHRIST'S HOSPITAL

ON THIS DAY, Sunday 19th May 2002, the School celebrated the move of Christ's Hospital from London to Horsham. This was also the centenary of the teaching of science in laboratories, or as H. E. Armstrong called them, 'workshops'. These centenaries were celebrated by an Open Day when parents, Old Blues, and others could visit the school, see exhibitions, listen to concerts or watch cricket. The boys and girls also had a free day.

The Head of Chemistry, Mrs Jenny Williams, asked me if I would give one of three talks on the teaching of chemistry. I said I thought that the visitors would rather watch cricket. However, I offered to give a demonstration class showing how I used to teach chemistry over half a century ago. Jenny thought this was a good idea and provided me with the necessary apparatus and a class of about fifteen volunteer pupils. About fifty or sixty adults stood at the back and we all enjoyed ourselves immensely (plate 17).

After the lesson was over Jenny remarked to me 'Of course we haven't time to do that sort of thing these days'. This made me very sad, but of course she was right. Most teachers will say that they do not have the time they used to have because so much has to be spent in filling up forms for the Department of Education. To do this, time and energy are required to make frequent assessments of students' ability and progress. This has never been easy. I remember when I first taught science at Christ's Hospital my head of department, D. H. Burleigh, warned me, when the time came to write 'reports' at the end of each term, to be brief. He himself seldom wrote more than 'Satisfactory', 'Very satisfactory', or 'Not satisfactory'. 'Don't write too much', he said, 'it only causes trouble'! These days the 'trouble caused' extends far beyond the consumption of teachers' time. It involves frequent tests, verbal or written, and affects the position of the school in the League Tables. League Tables may have had their uses in raising the general level of instruction in schools and in helping parents in choosing a school to which to send their kids, but they have potentially a disastrous effect on the process of education.

'A child's mind is not a vessel to be filled but a fire to be kindled'. Education is losing its way. The Prime Minister talks about 'an age of knowledge' when he should be aiming at 'an age of understanding'. Different objectives require different methods. If our aim is to 'fill vessels', methods using didactic lessons, cramming, league tables and examination of knowledge are suitable. But if our aims are to 'kindle fires' we must use discovery methods, abandon league tables and set examination questions that test understanding, not mere knowledge.

During World War II I had to take a party of cadets to a Royal Air Force station to learn how a machine gun works. A corporal laid out the machine gun on a table in front of us and proceeded to strip it down, naming the parts as he did so. He then said 'Any questions?' A cadet replied 'I don't understand how it fires'. The corporal replied 'It is fired by the gunner pressing his finger on the button'. 'Yes', said the cadet, 'but it is a machine gun – how does it continue to fire?' That was an easy one for the corporal: 'It continues to fire by the gunner keeping his finger pressed on the button'. That was 'instruction' – enough for the cadet to know how to fire the gun. But he still did not understand how it worked, and if anything went wrong and the gun did not fire he would have been unable to do anything about it.

That, in a simple episode, should explain the difference between 'knowledge' and 'understanding', between Instruction and Education.

If pupils go on to a college or university, teachers there frequently complain that they do not understand much of what they were taught and have a poor basis on which their university course can build. This is very similar to the situation that Professor Armstrong found when he was a university lecturer to engineering and medical students in the 19th century (See Chapter 2). The result was his emphasis on understanding expressed through his 'heuristic method' of school teaching. In describing this method in earlier chapters the concept of 'heuristic patches' has been referred to. It should still be possible, in spite of the general shortage of time, to find a week or so for a 'heuristic patch' occasionally – say once a term. Even that would be something to enlighten the pupils on how scientists work and of what processes of observation, hypothesising and experiment lie behind the bald statements in the textbook.

There are a few indications that teachers themselves are stirring against the impositions which force them to substitute Instruction for Education. I wrote a letter to *The Times* about this and it was published on July 16th, 2002:

True education has been replaced by instruction: do this, learn that and you will get high marks in GCSE, and your school will rise to a higher place in the league tables and you may go on to university studies for which you will not be adequately equipped, or to a routine job for which you will.

To restore true education will be a mammoth task requiring drastic measures. As a start the league tables must be abolished, alternatives to GCSE must be provided and examiners must set questions that test understanding and not merely knowledge.

At about the same time, Richard Dawkins, FRS, the distinguished biologist and Professor of the Public Understanding of Science at Oxford University, wrote an article in *The Guardian* which concluded with these words:

> Now, let's whip up a gale of reform through the country, blow away the assessment-freaks with their never-ending cycle of demoralising, childhood-destroying examinations, and get back to true education.

When these reforms eventually happen, as I believe they must, there will be teachers waiting in the wings, especially, I hope, at Christ's Hospital, ready to re-introduce discovery methods, not of course for teaching whole syllabuses but to enable pupils to experience, through short 'heuristic patches', how scientists tackle problems and to understand, as well as to learn, the material they are studying.

It seems to me to be a self-evident truth that children learn most easily when they find things out for themselves. Old Professor Armstrong's heuristic ideas are not outdated – discovery methods are still the most successful, and by far the most enjoyable, way to teach science.

In conclusion, I should like to add that in discussing the influence of Christ's Hospital on the teaching of science, I have tried to avoid bald statements of my opinion and to give chapter-and-verse evidence where possible. This will explain why so much space is given to Chapter 3 and why Chapter 13 gives quotations from the Malaysian Director General of Education to describe our Curriculum Development Project in Malaysia.

By recording these examples of the use of the discovery method of teaching science, derived from Professor Armstrong's heuristic method, I hope that present and future teachers of science will be reminded – in spite of frequent pressures to 'change the syllabus' in one direction or another and for one reason or another – to 'keep their eyes on the ball' and never forget that

> 'A child's mind is not a vessel to be filled but a fire to be kindled'
> (Plutarch).

REFERENCES

1. Browne, C. E.: *Henry Edward Armstrong. Educational Work*. The Chas. E. Browne Book Fund. 1954.
2. Rodd, E. H. *Charles E. Browne. An Appreciation of his Work for the Reform of Education at Christ's Hospital, 1899–1926*. The Charles E. Browne Book Fund. 1966.
3. Armstrong, H. E. *The Teaching of Scientific Method, and other papers on education.* London: Macmillan & Co. 1903.
4. Armstrong, H. E. *H. E. Armstrong and science education. Selections from 'The teaching of scientific method' and other papers on education by H. E. Armstrong.* Edited, with an introduction, by G. Van Praagh. London: John Murray. 1973.
5. Loutit, J. F. and Scott, O. C. A. Louis Harold Gray, 1905–1965. *Biog.Mem.Roy.Soc.Lond.*, **12** 195–216 (1966)
6. Van Praagh, G. *The Teaching of Science at Christ's Hospital Since 1900 A.D.* Crawley: Frognal Publishers. 1992.
7. Van Praagh, G. *Chemistry by Discovery*. London: John Murray. 1960.
8. Ainley, D. *The Adelie Penguin – Bellwether for climate change*. Columbia University. 2002.
9. Association for Science Education. *Chemistry for Grammar Schools*. John Murray. 1967.
10. Bradley, J. and Van Praagh, G. Reaction between potassium permanganate and oxalic acid and the decomposition of potassium permanganate. *J.Chem.Soc.* 1938: 1624–1636.
11. Anderson, D. J. and Van Praagh, G. Preliminary investigation of the temperatures produced in burring. *British Dental Journal* 1942, **73**:62-64.
12. Nuffield Science Teaching Project: O Level books. *Introduction and Guide; Handbook for Teachers; The Sample Scheme; Collected Experiments; Laboratory Investigations; Book of Data; Background Books; The Chemist in Action*. London: Longman/Penguin Books. 1966.
13. James, G. H. *A mechanistic introduction to organic chemistry*. London: Mills & Boon. 1968.
14. Vincent-Smith, C. and Hackett, R. Q. *A Practical Approach to Systems Electronics*. Longman. 1985.
15. Hackett, R. Q. *Inquiring into Physics*. Pergamon. 1972.
16. Hughes, Thea Stanley. *Ernest Giles explorer*. Movement Publications (Australia). 1988.
17. Van Praagh, G. *Seeing it Through: Travels of a Science Teacher*. Gatwick Press. 1988.
18. *Tun Hamdan Sheikh Tahir; His Life and Times as Seen by Himself and Others*. Based on the original version of Tun Hamdan's Biography 'Tun Hamdan: Guru Sepanjang Hayat' by Mohd. Nor Long. Translated and adapted with additional material by D. J. Muzaffar Tate. Malaysia: Persatuan Sejarah Malaysia. 2001.
19. Van Praagh, G. Practicals have not gone. *Education in Science*, 2000, **189**, 30.

SUBSCRIBERS

The publication of this book has been made possible by the generosity of donors. We wish to record our gratitude to Lord Simon, the Nuffield Foundation, the Salters' Company and the following former pupils of Dr Van Praagh:

B. E. Adams	R. A. Fennell	D. G. Porter
R. G. Adams	B. D. Hankin	P. F. Portwood
J. D. Asteraki	M. J. Heard	M. L. Reynolds
B. R. Aston	P. J. Hebben	D. P. Robinson
M. Bamford	C. L. Hicks	W. P. Robinson
C. J. Bates	J. M. Hinton	F. J. C. Rossotti
I. F. Bates	J. B. Hooper	C. Russell
R. D. Bates	E. P. G. Houssemayne Du Boulay	J. S. Sanders
J. V. Beer		B. Selton
M. P. Berry	R. J. S. Hudson	T. M. B. Silcock
S. K. Birch	J. D. A. Hutchings	R. H. Smith
R. M. Browne	C. A. Kirkman	A. W. D. Spackman
C. J. L. Buggé	D. J. Kluth	J. G. Spink
D. D. Carter	J. E. Kluth	C. G. Timms
M. R. Churchill	D. H. Lee	M. Waller
K. D. Clark	D. L. Marriott	R. H. Walter
I. Coward	P. D. Naylor	A. B. Watts
B. W. Cromie	I. E. C. Ounsted	J. R. West
J. S. Daniel	D. G. Parks-Smith	S. M. White
N. J. H. Dibben	T. R. Parsons	D. E. Wiggins
R. H. V. Dixon	J. K. Paterson	D. W. Willis
J. L. Doyle	D. A. Pearl	R. L. Woolley
J. S. Drury	M. J. Pitcher	R. M. Young

Thanks are also due to those at Christ's Hospital who assisted or supported the publication in other ways, in particular the Head Master, Dr Peter Southern; Dr Paul Maddren, Science Co-ordinator; Mrs Jenny Williams, Head of Chemistry; and Mr Mark Curtis and Ms Anne Sartain of the Partnership Office.

INDEX

Adams, Mrs xii
Aitchison College, Lahore viii, 1, 3, *pl* 4
Aitken, Kit 30
Allen, M. G. 17–18
Allsop, Terry 32, 37–40, 41, 50, 57
Anderson Prof. D. J. 16, 48, 49
Archbold, Tom 23
Armstrong, Prof. Henry E. vii, ix, xi, xiii, 4, 5, 14, 32, 34, 35, 47, 106, 107, 108, *pl* 2
– Browne on 4–7, 47
– Fyfe on 7–8
Asfah, Mr 71
Asteraki, J. D. 18

Baillie, Ian 30
Barber, Mrs 26
Barlow, Miss Kate (Mrs Jarvis) 18
Beaven, P. R. ('Pop') 20, 22, 48
Behravesh, Mr 69
Berry, Martyn P. 19, 32
Blake, Rick 19
Bloomfield, Peter xii
Bolton, C. J. 19, 51
Boo, Dato Kum 94
Booth, Norman 65
Boucher, Nick 19
Bourton, Mrs xii
Bowen, Prof. Keith 16, 19, 49
Bowles, John 38
Bradley, John 14, 33
British Council, The xi, 1, 68, 70, 73, 74, 76–7, 78, 79, 80, 81, 83, 84, 85, 86, 87, 99, 101
– Kampala Conference 86
Brotherton, Peter 58, 59
Brown, Dr Farrer 53
Brown, R. F. J. 27
Browne, Charles E. vii, ix, xi, xiii, 4, 13, 14, 15, 24, 32–4, 45, *pl* 3
– on Armstrong 4–7
– CH appointment 6
– CH *Science Journal*, letter to 47–8

– Fyfe on 8
– Pemberton on 24
– Rodd on 8–11
– Wallis on 13
Buggé, C. J. L. 20
Burleigh, Douglas H. 14, 24, 26, 45, 106
Bywater, Keith 19

Campbell, J. Arthur 65
Centre for Educational Development Overseas (CEDO) xii, 81, 86, 101
– VP Reports to 101,
– example of 102–5
Chaundy, David 32, 34–6
Chemistry by Discovery (book) 19, 36, 38, 39, 43, 55, 58, 65, 93, 100
Chemistry by Investigation (film) 38
Cheow, Brian 30, 78
Chisman, Dennis 79
Christ's Hospital
– Armstrong appointed to Council of 5, 32
– Centenary of Science 2002 viii, 106, *pl* 17
– 'heuristic' science teaching at vii, ix, xi, **4–14**, 15, 16, 31, 32–3, 37, 40, 45–6, 106–9
– 50th anniversary of 45
– large research projects 51–2
– Horsham, move to 9
– Nuffield O & A level at 40, 57, 58, 60
– pupils' notebooks 1902 10
– Report of Royal Commission on viii, 5
– Riches Lecture Theatre 59
– Salters' School of Chemistry 60
– *Science Journal* 23, 45, 46–7, *pl* 6
– articles from 47–51
– *Teaching of Science at, The, Since 1900* 16
Churchill, Prof. M. R. 20
Compton, Jim 28
Coulson, Ernest 55
Court, Charles 63
Cox, P. A. 20, 51
Crosland, Ronald, 22, 24, 26
Curr, C. 20–1
Curriculum Renewal and Educational

Development Overseas (CREDO) 74, 79–89
– Kampala Conference 86
– Malaysian Project 91–6
– Nairobi Conference 84–6
Curtis, Mark 111

Daniel, Sir John 19, 21
Davis, Peter 74, 86
Dawkins, Prof. Richard 108
Dickson, Murray 74
Doyle, John L. 21–2
Drury, J. S. 17

East African School Science Project 38, 41, 80, 83-9, 101–2, *pl 5*
Evans, P. 22
Exploring Chemistry (film) 45, 57

Flecker, H. L. O. viii, 2, 30, *pl 1*
– letter from Pakistan 1
Fletcher, C. G. 83
Florey, John 32, 38, 40–2, 86
Forajalla, Sibrino 30–1
Franklin, Prof. K. C. T. 15
Frost, Robert 21
Fyfe, Sir William Hamilton
– on Armstrong 7–8

Giles, Ernest 63
Gray, Dr L. H. 15, 49, 50
Greene, P. D. 22
Gribble, Dr 63
Guest, Michael xii

Hackett, Dr Roger 60
Hall, Prof. P. 15
Halliwell, Frank 37, 53, 54
Hamdan, Tan Sri Haji, Dr 90–1, 93, 98, *pl 10*
– on teaching science in Malaysia (CREDO project) 91–6
Harvey, Miss Elizabeth 18
Healey, Colin 64
Hooper, J. B. 22
Hornsby, Reggie 64
Hoskins, Dr Trevor xii, 23, 47, 48
Hutchings, Denis 24
Hyde, 'Dido' 15

James, Glyn 57, 58, 60
Jarvis, Mr 18
Jenkins, Edgar 32–4

Jones, M. B. 26

Kirby, Bill 20, 23, 28, 50

Lang, Dr 27
Lawrence, A. S. C. 12
Learning Science in Malaysia (film) 96, *pl 14*
Leiston, Prof. 88
Lewis, John 54
London Day Training College ix, 13, 32, 44

Maddren, Dr Paul 60, 111
Malaysia, Secondary Science Project 80, 81, 101–2, 108, *pls 8, 10–16*
– *Learning Science in Malaysia* (film) 96, *pl 14*
– Reports, example of 102–5
Malone, Stanley 59, 60
Mansell, Tony xi
Mappin, Ken 64
Matthews, Peter 18
McKeown, Paul 62
McLean, Prof. A. 16–17, 23
Meiklejohn 5
Messel, Dr 64
Ministry of Overseas Development 80, 81
see also British Council
Mitchell, Jack 56
Mitchell, John & Susan xii
Morpurgo, Prof. J. E. 43
Morris, Robert 79, 80, 81, 83, 84, 95
Mortimer, Helen 79
Moss, Stan 87
Mott, Sir Neville 54
Mwendwa, Mr 83, 84

Nasir (Azudin) 31
Newsome, David 58
Nichol, Robert 76
Northcott, Prof. D. G. 16
Nuffield Foundation 36, 38, 79, 81, 111
– O & A Level courses 35–6, 39, 57, 58, 60
– Science Teaching Project ix, xi, 33, 37, 38, 39, 41, 50, **53–61**, 62, 79, 93, 97
Nunn, Sir Percy xi, 44
Nyholm, Prof. Sir Ronald 54

Onn, Datuk Hussein 91
Open University, The 21
Ounsted, Dr Christopher 46
Parks-Smith, D. 24, 51
Pelmore, Denis 57–8, 59

INDEX

Pemberton, Prof. J. 24
Porter, George, Lord 38, 60
Potter, Fiona xii, xiii
Poulton, Richard xii
  – foreword by vii–ix

Quraishi, A. R. viii, 1, 2, 3, *pls 1, 4*

Rawlins, Rev. Douglas 75
Reuben, Mosko 30, 75
Reynolds, Lance xii, 25
Roberts, D. S. 2, 28
Roberts, Harry 64
Robinson, Prof. W. P. 25–6
Rodd, Ernest H. 4
  – on Browne 8–11
  – on Record books 11–12
Rossotti, F. J. C. 26, 28
Royal Society, The 5, 15, 32
Ruthven D. M. 26

St John's University, Shanghai 13
Salters' Company 111
  – Advanced Chemistry Courses 40
  – Prize: Teaching of Chemistry 60
  – School of Chemistry at CH 60
Sartain, Anne 111
Seakins, Michael 27, 48
Sills, Harry 18, 26
Simon, David, Lord 111
Sinker, Sir Paul 101
Sladen, W. J. L. 27
Smith, Sir Ewart 12, 15
Southern, Dr Peter 111
Steward, John 86
Stokes, Bryan 32, 36–7
subscribers to this book 111

Taplin, Prof. D. M. R. 28
Tarimu, Cuthbert 80, 83, 84
Todd, Lord 53

UNESCO 86, 89

Van Praagh, Dr Gordon
  – Centenary Day at CH viii, 106, *pl 17*
  – *Chemistry by Discovery* (book) 19, 36, 38, 39, 43, 55, 58, 65, 93, 100
  – CEDO, Reports to 101, 102–5
  – CREDO appointment 79
  – Dato award Malaysia ix
  – Nuffield appointment 38, 53, 57
  – *Teaching of Science at Christ's Hospital Since 1900, The* (book) 16
  – work in
    – Africa, East & Central 79, 83–9, 101, *pl 9*
    – Australia, New Zealand 62–7
    – Hong Kong 81
    – Indonesia 81
    – Iran 68–72, *pl 7*
    – Lahore 1–3, *pl 4*
    – Malaysia 90–8, 101, *pls 8, 11–15*
    – Penang 97–100, *pl 16*
    – Sarawak 73–6
    – Seychelles 81–2
    – Singapore 76–8
    – Thailand viii
Veasey, T. 51–2
Verdin, A. 17, 28
Vincent-Smith, Christopher 58, 60

Wales, HRH Prince of 11
Wallis, Dr (Sir) Barnes 13, 15, 28, 49
White, Patrick 46
Williams, Dr E. C. 9
Williams, Mrs Jenny 106, 111
Willis, Donald W. 29

Yates, Prof. 87
Yiew, Dato Lim Cheong (later Tan Sri) 98
Yong, Stephen 73
Young, Brian 79
Yu, Ms Wei 21

Zeeman, Prof. Sir Christopher 16